Winning SBIR/STTR Grants:

A Ten-Week Plan for Preparing Your NIH Phase I Application

Eva Garland Consulting, LLC

ISBN: 8644300907
ISBN-13: 979-8644300907

CONTENTS

    1.1. Conduct a self-evaluation to determine if your project is ready for an SBIR/STTR application.
    1.2. Select the NIH Institute(s) or Center(s) and Scientific Review Groups (SRGs) most appropriate for your project.
    1.3. Download the Application Guide.
    1.4. Initiate all registrations.

    2.1. Prepare an initial outline of your budget, identify all work that will be done at outside institutions, and arrange for quotations and support letters.
    2.2. Finalize your team of researchers and consultants, and begin preparing Biographical Sketches.
    2.3. Compose your Title.
    2.4. Request Letters of Support from consultants, key opinion leaders, subaward PI(s), and/or potential customers.
    2.5. Contact Program Officer(s).

    3.1. Review the competitive landscape for your product.
    3.2. Assess whether you will be required to include information for Vertebrate Animals and/or Human Subjects.

    4.1. Identify references to include in your Significance and Innovation sections.
    4.2. Identify references to include in your Approach section.
    4.3. Complete follow-ups from conversations with PO(s).

    5.1. Prepare to write your Research Plan.
    5.2. Write the Significance section of your Research Strategy.
    5.3. Write the Innovation section of your Research Strategy.

11.2. Obtain your impact score and Summary Statement.
11.3. Receive your Notice of Award (or work on your resubmission).

FOREWORD
by Eva Garland, Ph.D.

Congratulations! You are about to embark on a highly proven path to funding the development of innovative technologies in the United States. Over the past 28 years, the **Small Business Innovation Research** (SBIR) and **Small Business Technology Transfer** (STTR) programs have awarded over $40 billion to small businesses. These grants have provided key seed funding for notable companies such as Genentech, Amgen, and Genzyme. SBIR/STTR grants from the National Institutes of Health (NIH) have resulted in hundreds of successfully commercialized products, including therapeutics, diagnostics, medical devices, and educational materials. These products incorporate new technologies that have dramatically improved quality of life, stimulated the economy through billions of dollars of revenue, and supported tens of thousands of talented scientists.

The SBIR/STTR program exists to help small businesses transition innovative ideas into commercial products. SBIR/STTR grants can play a critical role in a small business' overall financing strategy because they can fund highly innovative projects that are deemed too risky for Angel Investors or Venture Capitalists. Both new and established companies can benefit from SBIR/STTR funding to advance Research and Development (R&D) through the high-risk early stages. In 2012, the US Small Business Association (SBA) issued a rule allowing participation in the program for the first time by companies financed predominantly by institutional investors, thereby greatly expanding the number of companies and innovative projects that are eligible for funding through the program. Of course, this has also increased the competition to receive an award!

My experience with the SBIR/STTR program began in 2008. I was consulting for a startup company in North Carolina that had been founded in 2007 and was burning through its first round of financing very quickly, with no hope for additional investments due to the recession. I was searching the internet for funding options and came across the SBIR/STTR program. While other funding mechanisms we were exploring at the time required us to either provide ownership in the company (equity investments) or needed to be paid back (loans), the SBIR/STTR funding was very appealing since the money arrives in the form of a grant that never has to be paid back.

I wrote my first STTR proposal in December of 2008, and it was funded for $150,000. In the subsequent five years, I was responsible for SBIR/STTR proposal submissions as Vice President of Research & Development at a small biotech company which resulted in eleven SBIR/STTR awards for a total of $4.5 million. This funding represented the vast majority of the company's income from 2009-2013 and enabled the company's R&D program to thrive during a historically challenging period for raising capital.

During those years, I learned the ins and outs of the SBIR/STTR program, benefitted greatly from the advice of SBIR/STTR program staff and reviewers, and ultimately figured out the key ingredients of a successful proposal. I did most of this by muddling through various websites, attending conferences, and asking for advice from experienced SBIR/STTR recipients. However, I was never able to identify a single resource that outlined all of the aspects of putting together a successful NIH SBIR/STTR proposal. The purpose of this book is to fill that void.

This book will walk you through the detailed process of preparing and submitting an <u>NIH SBIR/STTR Phase I proposal</u>. One of the most common reasons people cite for NOT applying for SBIR/STTR funding is the overwhelming nature of the application process, and how it will detract from other business activities. Therefore, we have aimed to provide a highly organized approach for preparing a proposal over a 10-week time period that is not all-consuming, so that you can continue to conduct normal day-to-day business activities while working on your proposal. The total time required for preparing your proposal according to this plan is 150 hours, and your weekly effort will range from 10-25 hours. The objectives and tasks for each week are listed at the beginning of each chapter. For each task, the notation ">>" is used to indicate a specific job that you must complete, and the notation "□" is used to indicate a portion of the job.

Even if you follow the organized approach outlined in this book, you will likely find the proposal preparation process to be challenging and even frustrating at times. It is therefore helpful to remind yourself of the end-goal. First, the payoff for a Phase I grant is approximately $250,000 (or more) of non-dilutive funds, which provides you with more than $1,600 for each hour of time spent working on your proposal – a pretty good return on investment (ROI) for an early-stage project! Furthermore, your Phase I money should be considered a steppingstone to your Phase II award, which will provide substantially more funding, in the range of $1,500,000 (or more). Additionally, once you have successfully written one SBIR/STTR proposal, you will be able to prepare subsequent proposals much more quickly. By choosing your proposal topics carefully, you can potentially carry several SBIR/STTR awards simultaneously, providing millions of dollars in annual revenue for your company. So, your initial 150 hours of investment may lead to millions of dollars of annual return for several years! This is not just a hypothetical proposition, as many of our clients have experienced just such a scenario.

NIH SBIR/STTR Program. The **National Institutes of Health** is the second largest SBIR/STTR granting agency (after the Department of Defense (DOD)) and awards more than $1.1 billion each year to small businesses through the program. Companies generally enter the program by writing a Phase I proposal for approximately $250,000 for a project that is about 12 months long. Once you have been awarded a Phase I grant and have achieved the Specific Aims outlined in your Phase I project, you may apply for a Phase II grant for approximately $1.5 million that will typically fund two years of subsequent product development. You may also apply to the Fast-Track program, which minimizes the transition time between your Phase I and Phase II projects. While this is appealing, the Fast-Track mechanism is usually not recommended for first-time applicants due to the additional proposal requirements.

SBIR vs. STTR. The SBIR and STTR programs are similar in most respects. The main difference between these funding mechanisms is that the STTR program requires the company to have a partnering research institution, which must be awarded a minimum of 30% of the total grant funds. Also, the Principal Investigator (PI) for an STTR project may be employed by either the partnering research institution or the small business, while the PI for an SBIR project must be employed at least 51% by the small business at the time of award. If your company is a spin out from a university, an STTR proposal may be a good choice since an academic founder can be the PI for the grant. The disadvantage of an STTR award is that less of the total funds are allocated to the small business. As of this writing, a firm owned predominantly by institutional investors may only participate in the NIH SBIR program and not in the NIH STTR program.

Eligibility. Only for-profit small businesses (<500 employees) located in the United States and with majority US ownership are eligible to receive SBIR/STTR funding. Until 2013, companies were required to be owned at least 51% by individuals, and so predominantly institutionally owned firms were ineligible. However, the National Defense Authorization Act for Fiscal Year 2012 permitted up to 25% of SBIR funds to be awarded to small businesses that are more than 49% owned by institutional investors. The NIH was one of the first agencies to open up eligibility to small businesses owned predominantly by institutions, beginning with the 2013 fiscal year. The impact of the new rules will be monitored carefully over the next several years, and the regulations may be adjusted accordingly. More detailed eligibility rules can be found in the **Application Guide**, which you will review during Week 1 of the proposal writing process to confirm your company's eligibility for the SBIR/STTR program.

Proposal submission. We recommend that you submit your proposal using the NIH-sponsored **Application Submission System & Interface for Submission Tracking (ASSIST).** Prior to using ASSIST, you will create an account in **eRA Commons**, the electronic research administration website used by the NIH (see Week 1 for information on creating these accounts). Your final submission will consist of approximately 50 pages of material, including administrative information, the Research Plan, the Budget, Biographical Sketches, Letters of Support, facilities information, and other supporting documents. By far the most important part of your application is the seven-page Research Plan consisting of your Specific Aims and Research Strategy, which will be discussed in detail in later chapters. You will create PDF versions of each section of the proposal and upload the documents into ASSIST. Then, you will submit your proposal by providing your **Grants.gov** Authorized Organization

Representative (AOR) login information. Once your proposal is submitted, you can monitor its status in eRA Commons.

The review process. Your proposal will be assigned to a **Scientific Review Group (SRG)** (also referred to as a "Study Section") as well as one or more **NIH Institute(s) or Center(s) (IC(s))** within a few weeks after you submit your application. The SRG consists of approximately 30 peer reviewers from academia, clinical practice, and industry. Typically, three reviewers will be assigned to review your proposal in detail. They will provide a numerical score from 1-9 (1 being the best) in five categories: **Significance, Innovation, Approach, Investigator(s), and Environment**. Each reviewer will then provide a score for overall impact, which may not *necessarily* be an average of the category scores. If your average score for overall impact from these three initial reviewers ranks in the top half of applicants, then your proposal will be discussed at the SRG meeting in which all reviewers meet for a 1-2 day session. The SRG meeting occurs approximately 2 months after you submit your grant, and the review dates will be posted in eRA Commons. At the review session, the top half of proposals will be discussed by the entire panel, and each reviewer will score the overall impact of your grant between 1 and 9. Next, the scores will be averaged and then multiplied by 10, and you will receive an impact score (also referred to as an "impact/priority" score) between 10 and 90. The impact score is the most important factor in determining whether your proposal will be funded. Many ICs will publish a payline that establishes the impact score you must achieve in order for the grant to be funded (i.e., your score must be equal to or lower than the payline). If your grant scores extremely well, it may be funded within a couple of months of the review panel meeting; if your score is borderline, you may have to wait several months to find out if it is funded. A summary of the overall timeline for the grant application process is provided below.

Timing. As you can see from the timeline, one of the main disadvantages of the SBIR/STTR program is the time lapse between the proposal submission and the funding decision, as it can take up to 9-12 months after you submit your proposal to receive your funding notification.

Contacts. Three NIH staff are assigned to each proposal submission. The main scientific contact for your proposal is your **Program Officer (PO).** You should reach out to POs early on to obtain feedback on your proposed project (discussed further in Week 2). After your proposal is reviewed, your PO will provide insight on its likelihood of being funded. If you receive an award, you will communicate with your PO throughout your project period to discuss your scientific progress and preparation of your Phase II application. The **Scientific Review Officer (SRO)** is your main contact through the peer review process. The SRO will assign your application to reviewers and monitor the SRG. It is unlikely you will need to contact your SRO unless you have problems with your submission or questions about the review process. The **Grants Management Specialist (GMS)** oversees the financial aspects of your award. If you are being considered for an award, your GMS will provide you with a list of **Just in Time (JIT)** documentation required for the award and will evaluate whether your company's financial system has appropriate controls in place to receive federal funding.

Common misconceptions. We have found that there are several common misconceptions that potential candidates have about the NIH SBIR/STTR program, which can dissuade potentially strong applicants from submitting a successful application. Six common misconceptions are addressed below:

Misconception #1. I can't write a strong proposal in the 6 pages allotted for the Research Strategy

It is certainly overwhelming to try to fit a year's worth of proposed research into 6 pages. However, there are a number of tricks you can use to write a strong proposal within the page limitations. For example, while your Research Strategy is limited to 6 pages, your entire application will be approximately 50 pages. So, you can be creative about including information relevant to the Research Strategy in other documents (such as the Biographical Sketches or Facilities & Other Resources sections). You can also use references to support statements, which will enable you to limit the amount of detail you include in your text. Learning to use these and other tricks discussed in this book will provide you with a competitive advantage over other applicants who are less efficient at using the allotted space.

Misconception #2. "High risk" means I should propose a project that has high risk of failure.

The SBIR/STTR program often touts the program's focus on funding high-risk research that is too early for institutional investors to consider funding. However, the SBIR/STTR program ultimately wants the technologies that it funds to succeed, so the level of risk tolerance is generally moderate rather than high. We have found that nearly all successful proposals have supportive preliminary data, so that the technology is substantially de-risked prior to receiving SBIR/STTR funding. Due to the competitiveness of the SBIR/STTR program, it is extremely unlikely that you will receive funding based solely on a good idea; you should have supporting documentation, either generated internally or from literature citations, to validate that your idea has a reasonable chance of being successfully commercialized.

Misconception #3. My business is too small to be competitive.

Over half of all SBIR/STTR awards are granted to firms with fewer than 25 people, and one-third of awards are granted to firms with fewer than 10 people. Therefore, even very small companies have a good chance of receiving funding if they submit a high-quality proposal. The SBIR/STTR mechanism is a great way for new and extremely small companies to add staff and support early stages of product development. Even if your company does not yet have a physical location, you can apply for SBIR/STTR funding and move into a brick-and-mortar location at the time of award.

Misconception #4. The SBIR program is more favorable for small businesses than the STTR program.

While the SBIR program receives a larger total dollar amount than the STTR program (3.2% compared to 0.45% of the NIH extramural research budget), far more SBIR proposals are submitted than STTR proposals, and historically, paylines have been similar for both of these programs. Some applicants mistakenly think the STTR program is less favorable for small businesses because they have heard that the university will serve as the prime applicant and/or retain more intellectual property than with an SBIR project. For both SBIR and STTR projects that involve university partnerships, the small business will need to establish a formal agreement with the university regarding intellectual property, and the company will serve as the prime applicant. Your decision on which program to apply for should be based on which mechanism is a better fit for your project, and this depends on where the majority of the work will be performed, who will be the PI, and how the budget will be allocated.

Misconception #5. Phase I NIH SBIR/STTR awards are limited to $150,000.

While the SBA guideline for Phase I SBIR/STTR award amounts is $150,000, the NIH routinely funds Phase I proposals up to approximately $250,000. The budget can be even higher when you are addressing certain special topics, allowing for budgets ranging from $300,000 to $700,000. You will need to justify the need for the higher funding amount, but in our experience, asking for more funds has not negatively impacted the review process and ultimately provides you with more resources to successfully complete your Phase I objectives. If you plan to request more than the current NIH hard budget cap, it is important to discuss your budget with your PO prior to submission.

Misconception #6. SBIR/STTR grants only fund research and won't help with my other business expenses.

When you receive an SBIR or STTR grant, you will receive three "buckets" of money, which will be discussed in greater detail in Week 7. The **direct costs** consist of approximately 60% of the total funds, and these must be spent directly on research activities related to your project. You will also be awarded **indirect costs** and a **fee** that may be used for other business expenses. Indirect costs and fees represent one of the hidden benefits of the SBIR/STTR program, and by managing your money carefully, it may be possible to fund the majority of your business expenses with SBIR/STTR grants.

Ready to get started? Now that you have a good overview of what to expect throughout the NIH SBIR/STTR application process, you are ready to embark on the 10-week Phase I proposal preparation plan detailed in this book. So, let's jump into Week 1!

Authors' Note

The NIH frequently changes its URLs for accessing necessary web-based material. Therefore, we have not included URLs for web pages that you will need to access to prepare and submit your application. Instead, we have provided search terms so that you can find the pages through internet search engines, and we maintain an updated list of relevant links on our book website, **evagarland.com/books**. We also recommend that you access the NIH SBIR/STTR website often for updates, and it is a good idea to subscribe to the NIH SBIR/STTR LISTSERV.

ACKNOWLEDGEMENTS

The SBIR/STTR program exists to fund innovative technologies, yet the SBIR/STTR program itself is an example of a great American innovation. Therefore, we first and foremost acknowledge those forward-thinking individuals who conceived of the SBIR/STTR program nearly three decades ago, as well as our current legislators who recognize the important role the SBIR/STTR program plays in supporting and accelerating development of new technologies in the United States. As those involved in the SBIR/STTR program acutely realize, innovations funded by the program provide a clear and direct benefit to humankind through the development of new technologies that greatly enhance our lives.

Secondly, we would like to acknowledge the superb individuals who administer the NIH SBIR/STTR program, which is one of the most efficient and well-run federal programs we have encountered. This comes from the diligence and excellence of many individuals within the program. NIH SBIR/STTR staff, especially Program Officers, have shared a wealth of knowledge with us not only about the NIH SBIR/STTR program but also about the nuances involved in translating great technologies from concept to commercialization. It is unusual for a program of this magnitude to possess such a friendly and helpful culture, and we thank the entire NIH SBIR/STTR staff.

We are grateful to our clients who have shared their exciting technologies with us and who have entrusted us with the responsibility of helping them create winning research proposals so that they can advance their innovations through the initial stages of research and development.

The third edition of this book benefits from the contributions of dozens of talented individuals who have written, read, and re-read either portions of the book or its entirety. Dr. Angela Pollard led the project, challenging us to think carefully about all aspects of the content and presentation and to meet aggressive deadlines, all while making the process seem fun! Dr. Lindsay Tanskey, Dr. Lara Skwarek, Dr. Chris Showell, Dr. Tiger Xie, and Dr. Jessica Lerch contributed valuable content and editing. Dr. Wout Salenbien provided our cover design and navigated the technical aspects of publishing the manuscript.

Finally, we thank our family, friends, and Eva Garland Consulting colleagues for their support throughout the writing of this book.

Winning SBIR/STTR Grants:
A Ten-Week Plan for Preparing Your
NIH Phase I Application

WEEK 1
Time required: 20 hours

Objectives

In this first week of preparing your Phase I proposal, you will determine whether your idea has a reasonable chance of being funded through the NIH SBIR/STTR program by conducting a self-evaluation. Then, you will evaluate which NIH Institute(s) and Center(s) (ICs), as well as which Scientific Review Groups (SRGs), will be the best fit for your project. Next, you will download and read relevant sections of the ~170 page NIH SBIR/STTR Application Guide to prepare yourself for the proposal preparation work that lies ahead. Finally, you will initiate all the registrations that are necessary in order for you to submit your proposal.

Tasks

1.1. Conduct a self-evaluation to determine if your project is ready for an SBIR/STTR application.

1.2. Select the NIH Institute(s) or Center(s) and SRGs most appropriate for your project.

1.3. Download the Application Guide.

1.4. Initiate all registrations.

1.1. Conduct a self-evaluation to determine if your project is ready for an SBIR/STTR application.

Before embarking on your 150-hour proposal preparation effort, you should ensure that your project has a reasonable chance of being granted an award. This section describes how to perform a self-evaluation on the key metrics by which NIH SBIR/STTR proposals are evaluated, namely: Significance, Innovation, Approach, Investigator(s), and Environment. We recommend you keep an electronic journal with the answers to these self-evaluation questions, as you can use your written responses as a starting point for an outline when you are ready to write your proposal.

Metric #1: Significance

Your proposal must address a significant <u>unmet</u> medical need. You should not simply propose an alternative to an existing solution but must be able to clearly identify a medical <u>problem</u> that currently has <u>no solution</u>. A new therapy for a disease that is already treatable with current therapies is unlikely to be funded. However, if you can show that current therapies do not work sufficiently, or that their efficacy is decreasing, e.g., due to resistance development, then you have a good case for the significance of your idea. It is advantageous to address a problem that affects a large number of people, such as HIV/AIDS or cancer, but be sure to be realistic in what problem your technology will truly solve. It is unlikely reviewers will believe that you are able to "cure cancer;" however, a new therapy to improve treatment outcomes for a form of cancer with high morbidity/mortality rates would be viewed favorably.

>> Perform the following self-evaluation to assess the significance of your idea:

☐ Will your project directly lead to the development of a specific product, or is it more focused on fundamental research? For the SBIR/STTR program it is critical for your project to lead to a well-defined product as opposed to building a platform technology for multiple applications.

☐ What is the <u>unmet</u> medical need that your product will address? Be quantitative and realistic in stating the number of patients, healthcare workers, etc. who have a need for the product you are developing.

☐ Which segment(s) of the population will benefit from your idea? Are there specific underserved groups, such as minorities, women, children, the economically disadvantaged, etc., who will benefit?

☐ In addition to medical benefits, what other economic and societal benefits will your technology provide? From an economic perspective, can you quantify the costs associated with the lack of currently available options (e.g., increased hospital time)? What are the direct and indirect benefits to society (e.g., enhanced quality of life or fewer days off work)?

☐ Which external factors support the need for your technology, such as changes in insurance reimbursement, an increasing population with disease X, or changes to the regulatory environment? You should be able to make a case for why your product should be developed <u>now</u> within the broader context of the current legal/societal/regulatory landscape.

□ What is the market opportunity for your product? If your product is successfully commercialized, who will buy it and why?

If you were able to answer the above questions with relative ease, and you feel confident that your technology addresses a significant unmet need, then you should move on to the next section. If you are unsure whether you can provide a strong answer to any of the above questions, you should consult with key opinion leaders and review relevant literature to ensure you have a solid value proposition. You should also bring up any questions about the significance of your project during the conversations with Program Officers (POs) that you will have in Week 2.

Metric #2: Innovation

The innovation of your project is evaluated based on the breakthrough potential of your technology. While incremental technological advances may lead to very lucrative commercial products and may form the basis of an outstanding business model, <u>incremental advancements are not appropriate for the NIH SBIR/STTR program</u>. Instead, SBIR/STTR grants are intended for technologies that are <u>highly innovative</u> and create a completely new direction for a field. Examples of low innovation and high innovation ideas are presented in the following table:

Incremental Projects (not likely to be funded by SBIR/STTR)	Innovative Projects (likely to be funded by SBIR/STTR)
Make minor structural modifications to an existing class of molecules to modestly improve potency, safety, etc.	Develop a new class of molecules with a novel mechanism of action to address a currently untreatable disease.
Improve an existing diagnostic device (making it easier to use, cheaper, etc.).	Develop a new diagnostic for a clear unmet need (allowing for earlier detection of important diseases, etc.).
Incrementally improve an existing drug delivery system by optimizing key parameters (e.g., particle size, polarity, etc.).	Develop a drug delivery system to reach a new therapeutic target that could not be previously accessed.

>> Objectively evaluate your project to determine if you are proposing an incremental advancement or if your product truly will result in a new direction for your field:

□ What are the existing state-of-the-art technologies in the field? Provide 3-4 bullet points on innovative technologies that have defined your field or that are currently being developed to solve the same problem.

□ How does your technology differ from the current state-of-the-art technologies in the field? Provide a minimum of three bullet points that clearly differentiate your product from others. Rank these in order of importance.

□ How will you protect your idea from copycats? Ideally, you have already filed a patent application, but you must at least have a solid plan for how you will protect your intellectual property once you reach key proof-of-concept milestones.

If you have trouble answering the above questions, the SBIR/STTR program is not appropriate for your idea, although you may want to think about ways to reformulate your proposal to enhance its innovation. Discussions with key opinion leaders or POs may be helpful in this regard. If your idea passes the high innovation metric, you are ready to consider the "nuts and bolts" sections of your proposal, starting with your research approach.

Metric #3: Approach

Although reviewers are supposed to place the most emphasis on the significance and innovation of your idea, they often will make the most comments about your research approach. Your Approach makes up the largest section of your Research Plan, and contains the most technical detail, so it is the easiest section for reviewers to criticize. Therefore, you will want to ensure that you develop a comprehensive scope of work to achieve relevant technical milestones. One of the main restrictions you face in formulating your proposal is that you must design a Research Plan that can be completed for approximately $150,000 (direct costs) with an endpoint consisting of one or more clear and relevant product development milestone(s).

Your Approach will typically consist of 1-3 Specific Aims, each with a defined technical milestone that is critical to achieve for the project to advance (i.e., a go/no-go decision point). As the name implies, each Specific Aim should be concrete and narrow in scope, and should have a clearly defined metric of success associated with it. Examples of strong Specific Aims include:

Specific Aim	Metric of Success
Evaluate a library of compounds for anti-coagulant activity using an *in vitro* assay.	The compounds must demonstrate statistically significant activity compared to a relevant control when used at concentrations ≤ 100 ppm.
Test mechanical stability of a new prosthetic device.	The device must endure forces 10x greater than those that would be exerted on it during normal use.
Correlate use of a new software system to decreased physician errors.	Physician error rates must be reduced by more than 20% using the new software compared to the old system.

A good resource for more examples of Specific Aims from successfully funded projects is the NIH Reporter website. This site provides the Title and Project Summary for all funded NIH projects. You can search for funded SBIR/STTR projects on topics that are similar to yours. Then, you can read the Project Summaries, as many proposals will explicitly list their Specific Aims in their Project Summaries.

>> You will now formulate a first draft of your Specific Aims, which will serve as the foundation for your Research Plan:

□ Create a list of milestones that must be achieved between now and commercialization of your technology, with associated timelines and costs for each item on the list. Hopefully, there will be a clear set of 1-3 early milestones that can be achieved for approximately $150,000. These milestones should not simply involve "turning the crank" projects, such as compound production, but should require a skilled R&D team to execute. Some good examples of milestones include synthesizing more potent derivatives of a lead compound or developing a beta-version of a new software product. These milestones will become the Specific Aims for your proposal.

>> For each of your Specific Aims, address the following questions:

□ What is the objective and how will you accomplish it?

□ What is the metric of success?

□ How will completion of your proposed Aim yield a key developmental milestone on your path to product commercialization?

Once you can answer each of the above questions, you have developed the foundation for your Approach, and you are ready to consider how you will go about executing your Research Plan, which will include building a strong team and identifying an appropriate environment.

Metric #4: Investigator(s)

The reviewers will evaluate whether you have assembled a team of investigators with expertise in all aspects of your proposed work and whether this team has a record of previous success. If you are at an established company with a history of commercializing products, assembling a proven team is generally a straightforward task. However, if you are the only person at your company and have limited connections to experts in your field, you will need to put a great deal of effort into assembling a team to convince reviewers that you and your co-investigators are capable of developing and commercializing your innovation.

The most important investigator is the Principal Investigator

(PI), who will lead the project. For an SBIR project, the PI must be an employee of the small business and must be at least 51% employed by the small business at the time of the award and throughout the project period. For an STTR project, the PI may be either an employee of the company or a collaborator at the partnering research institution. If your company does not have an employee with an established record in the field, applying for an STTR grant with an expert collaborator as the PI may strategically enhance your chance of success.

It is usually not possible for the PI to possess expertise in all areas needed to successfully execute your project, and a Phase I team generally consists of 3-10 individuals who fill various roles. Your team must include individuals who possess technical expertise in all areas of your proposed project, are experienced in product development, and can provide the perspective of the end-user (e.g., clinical expertise). You can be creative in how you build your team, and should consider including employees, consultants, collaborators, and/or contractors as key personnel for your project.

>> Establish your team of investigators and identify any gaps.

    □ Determine the characteristics of the team necessary to complete your proposed work.
        1) Area(s) of technical expertise (e.g., chemistry, molecular biology, toxicology, engineering).
        2) Area(s) of clinical expertise.
        3) Area(s) of commercial/regulatory expertise.

    □ Who will be your PI? Assess this individual's strengths and weaknesses in each of the areas identified above.

☐ Identify all areas of needed expertise that your PI does not possess. List any individuals you have already identified to fill these gaps.

☐ For all remaining gaps, determine how you will go about filling these required areas of expertise. You may need to cold call experts such as clinicians and university professors, and this should be done as early as possible. Keep in mind that contract research organizations (CROs) often have experts in-house who will be willing to provide their Biographical Sketches to include in your proposal, as long as you agree to use that CRO as a subcontractor on your project.

Metric #5: Environment

Your company is required to possess a physical facility for the project. However, this does not necessarily mean that you need to invest in expensive laboratory space. Some of the work that may require specialized facilities can be performed at an academic institution or at a CRO. The STTR mechanism is often a good choice for a company that does not have extensive facilities, as this will provide you with access to your partnering research institution's facilities.

>> Determine which facilities you will need for your project and devise a plan to secure these facilities.

☐ List all facilities and equipment needed to complete each Aim of your project. Make note of specialized equipment and facilities (GMP, BSL2, etc.) that will be required.

☐ Determine which facilities and equipment are already available for your use and which you will need to secure in order to complete the work in your Approach.

If you don't currently have all the facilities and equipment you will need to complete your project, you will need to do some scrambling! If a key equipment item is missing, you may purchase it as part of your project as long as you can fit it into your budget. For more expensive equipment, consider local academic institutions, which may have the equipment available and would be willing to charge on a pay-per-use basis. Another option is to use CROs, although they may be more expensive. You also could consider sharing space and/or equipment with another small business. If you have not yet secured the laboratory space that you will need for your project, you can state in the proposal that you have identified a space that will be leased once your Phase I grant is awarded.

You have now completed your self-evaluation. <u>Organize your responses to this self-evaluation in outline form and keep them handy, as you will refer to them throughout the proposal preparation process.</u>

1.2. Select the NIH Institute(s) or Center(s) and SRGs most appropriate for your project.

Once you submit your proposal, it will be assigned to one or more NIH IC(s) that will ultimately be responsible for funding your project, if it is awarded. At the time of submission, you will use the <u>PHS Assignment Request</u> form to request the IC(s) to which you would like your project assigned.

>> Browse the research topics that each IC considers to be high priority to determine which ICs are most appropriate for your project. You can find these research topics on the "Funding" page of the NIH SBIR/STTR website, under the link "Program Descriptions and Research Topics".

□ Conduct a keyword search for your research topic, and identify ICs that would likely have an interest in your project. Your idea does not need to fall within one of the specific topics listed; in fact, the NIH is known for its flexibility in funding a variety of topics, unlike other agencies such as the Department of Defense, who are very specific in the topics they will consider for SBIR/STTR funding.

□ Once you have identified one or more ICs that you feel would be appropriate for your project, note the name(s) of the Program Contacts listed with those relevant ICs. These will help you identify the correct POs for the ICs, and you will be contacting this PO in Week 2. If you feel there may be several ICs appropriate for your project, you are in the advantageous position of having several POs whom you may contact.

Many SBIR/STTR applicants incorrectly assume that your assigned NIH IC is also responsible for reviewing your proposal, but this is not the case. Your application will be assigned to an SRG, which consists of the individuals who will be reviewing and scoring your proposal. In your application PHS Assignment Request form, you have the opportunity to request the most appropriate SRG for your project, and you should put careful consideration into requesting an SRG that has a high probability of viewing your proposal favorably.

>> Search for "Small Business and Technology Transfer (SBIR/STTR) Study Section" on the NIH Center for Scientific Review website. You will access a list of approximately 35 SRGs that are responsible for reviewing SBIR/STTR proposals.

□ Click on each SRG that you feel may be relevant to your project to learn more about the topics covered by that SRG.

□ Once you have narrowed down your list to a few relevant SRGs, click on the Meeting Roster for prior meeting dates of each relevant SRG. The Meeting Roster will list all reviewers from prior review sessions, and you will likely recognize some of the names as experts in your field. Although you cannot know for sure which reviewers will be on the SRG when your proposal is reviewed, many reviewers serve several terms on the same SRG, so you can obtain a good idea of who may review your proposal.

□ Select the SRG that is most relevant for your proposal. Write this down, as you will include it in your <u>PHS Assignment Request</u> form, which you will fill out in ASSIST in Week 8. You can request up to 3 SRGs in your <u>PHS Assignment Request</u> form and they should be listed in order of preference.

□ If you need assistance in identifying appropriate SRGs, you can use the Assisted Referral Tool that is offered by NIH's Center for Scientific Review. The online tool will prompt you to enter your title and text from the application and will provide suggestions for SRGs.

You are selecting an SRG so early in the proposal writing process because the reviewers in the SRG are the audience for your proposal. By reviewing prior Meeting Rosters, you now have a good sense of the backgrounds of those who will review your proposal. You likely found the Meeting Roster to consist of an accomplished group of academic and industry professionals with expertise related to your proposed work. However, there were probably several members on the panel with only peripheral knowledge of your topic, so it is important to write your proposal in such a manner that people who are not experts in your field can understand and appreciate your proposed work.

1.3. Download the Grant Application Guide.

You will be referencing the SBIR or STTR Parent Funding Opportunity Announcement (FOA) frequently over the next several weeks, and so this is a good time to begin familiarizing yourself with it.

>> Identify the "<u>SBIR</u> Omnibus/Parent Funding Opportunity Announcement" or the "<u>STTR</u> Omnibus/Parent Funding Opportunity Announcement" link on the NIH SBIR/STTR website. These are found on the "Funding" page of the website. There are separate funding opportunities for grants that propose clinical trials and those that do not. <u>Make sure you choose the correct funding announcement for your project.</u>

□ When you click on the FOA, you will be directed to a site with several pages of text detailing the funding announcement. Read through this text to obtain an overview of the application requirements, as well as the review criteria.

□ In the FOA, under "Required Application Instructions", you will see a link for the SF 424 (R&R) SBIR/STTR Application Guide. Download and save this file in a convenient place. You will refer to the Application Guide frequently as you develop and submit your application.

□ The announcement will list several options for submitting your application. We recommend using the Application Submission System & Interface for Submission Tracking (ASSIST). ASSIST is a web-based portal that provides a user interface that allows you to create grant applications, upload sections of your grant, preview the full proposal, and submit your grant to the NIH.

We will discuss loading your grant application into ASSIST in future weeks, but for now, open the Application Guide. You may be surprised to find that the instructions are 170 pages long! The good news is that you do not need to read every page, and this book will provide a logical approach to reading the relevant sections as you prepare your application. *Throughout this book, we will italicize the relevant section when we refer to the Application Guide.*

>> Open the Application Guide.

□ We highly recommended that you save the Application Guide PDF in a convenient location on your computer. You will be referring to this document often over the next 10 weeks. Depending on your preference, you may wish to print the Application Guide. However, because it features many helpful Quick Links to help you navigate the document, and external hyperlinks to direct you to external resources and guidance, you may find the electronic version to be most helpful.

□ Carefully read the *Small Business Eligibility Criteria* that you can access through a link in the *Program Overview* section of the Application Guide. Clicking on the "Small Business Eligibility Criteria" link will take you to where this information is located on the NIH SBIR/STTR webpage. Read this section carefully to confirm that your company is eligible for SBIR and/or STTR funding. If you have any questions about your eligibility requirements, which are quite complicated, discuss your company's eligibility with a PO.

□ Skim all sections of the Application Guide to obtain a sense of the work that lies ahead. Skip sections that do not apply to you, such as Fast-Track and Supplemental Applications. You should spend no more than 1-2 hours completing this initial review of the Application Guide. We will start digging into these instructions in substantially more detail in the upcoming weeks!

☐ Obtain the Annotated Form Set by clicking on the "Annotated Form Sets" link under the Related Resources subheading in the Application Process section of the Application Guide. The Annotated Form Set will serve as an excellent visual to the application forms as you are completing the application in later weeks.

☐ As you will be referring to the Application Guide often through the upcoming weeks, here are some tips to help you navigate it:

- Use the "Bookmarks" feature in your PDF reader to quickly navigate to the different sections of the Application Guide.
- Use the "Quick Links" located in each section (marked by headers in dark gray boxes) to efficiently navigate to relevant subheadings (marked by headers in blue boxes).
- Use the Ctrl+F or Command+F function on your computer to search for relevant keywords.
- Use the hyperlinks located throughout the Application Guide to reference current NIH guidance and other helpful resources. For example, the "Format Attachments" link will take you the NIH webpage with details about page limits, citations, acceptable font sizes, and other formatting requirements. Other hyperlinks are provided to help you locate registration websites, sample Biographical Sketches, standard due dates, and more.

1.4. Initiate all registrations.

There are several registrations that must be completed before you can access ASSIST in order to initiate, and eventually submit, your application. Some of these registrations take several days to complete, so it is a good idea to take care of these early in your proposal preparation process.

>> Initiate the registrations required for your proposal submission.

☐ Obtain a **DUNS number** from Dun & Bradstreet (D&B). This is a unique 9-digit number that aids the NIH in identifying your company, and it can be obtained for free in one day from the D&B website. There is a link to the NIH "Register" webpage in the *Application Process* section of the Application Guide. Visit this site for detailed information about obtaining a DUNS number and initiating the other required registrations. Once you are on the "Register" webpage, click the "Organization/Organization Representative Registration" link for guidance.

Registrations frequently change. For example, at the time of this writing, the DUNS number is in the works of being replaced by a Unique Entity Identifier (UEI). Refer to the current Application Guide regarding updated registration information.

☐ Register your company in the **System for Award Management (SAM)**. This registration is required for all companies to receive funds from the Federal Government. It may take up to six weeks after you apply to receive your SAM registration. The link to the NIH "Register" webpage in the *Application Process* section of the Application Guide will direct you to detailed information about completing your SAM registration. SAM uses Login.gov to allow you to sign in to your account; therefore, the first step in setting up your company's SAM registration is to create an account with Login.gov. Registration with SAM is free. **Be aware that there are several websites that will attempt to charge you for registering with SAM; make sure you do not get scammed by these sites.**

☐ Register your company with **Grants.gov**, which is the mechanism the Federal Government uses for grant announcements and applications. Once you have finished preparing your proposal in ASSIST, you will need to enter an Authorized Organization Representative (AOR) login and password for Grants.gov in order to complete the final submission step. You must have a DUNS number and have completed your SAM registration before registering with Grants.gov. Use the link to the NIH "Register" webpage in the *Application Process* section of the Application Guide for detailed information about completing your Grants.gov registration. Go to the Grants.gov website and click "register" at the upper right of the window. Choose "Get Registered Now," and enter your information. A temporary code will be emailed and must be entered to continue. Choose the "Add Organization Applicant Profile" option to affiliate your account with the company. Enter the company's DUNS number or UEI, your profile name, and job title. An email will be sent to the Electronic Business Point of Contact (eBiz POC) designated in SAM. Carefully follow the instructions sent by Grants.gov. After completing the registration, you can use your Grants.gov eBiz POC account to assign roles for your company. One of these roles will be the AOR, and the AOR's Grants.gov username and password will be required to submit your grant application in ASSIST.

☐ Create an eRA Commons account for your company and for your PI. The NIH uses eRA Commons to track grant applications, and you will access this site often over the next several months to view the status of your application. The link to the NIH "Register" webpage in the *Application Process* section of the Application Guide can direct you to detailed information about completing your eRA Commons registration. You must first "Register Grantee Organization". Your registration information must be reviewed and approved before you are provided a temporary password to set up your account. You will then create a new password, carefully review the company's information, and electronically sign the request for the account to become active in eRA Commons. This first user account will be designated the entity's Signing Official (SO). The SO will be responsible for the administrative aspects of your grant, such as submitting pre-award and post-award documents once your grant has been recommended for funding. Next, register your PI in eRA Commons and associate this individual with your company. If your company has only a few employees, it is often simplest to have the same person serve as PI and the SO. Even though the same person may be both the PI and the SO, you need to create separate eRA Commons accounts for each role. For simplicity, you may wish to add "SO" to the end of the login name for the account with the SO role. It is especially important that you carefully follow all of the instructions on the NIH "Register" webpage for registering in eRA Commons because if you make any mistakes during the registration process, you will be frustrated later on when you attempt to submit your application.

☐ Your company will need to register with the Small Business Administration (SBA) through the SBIR website (sbir.gov).

When you register, you will receive a nine-digit Small Business Concern (SBC) Control ID that you will enter in your grant application. The link to the NIH "Register" webpage in the *Application Process* section of the Application Guide can direct you to detailed information about completing your SBA registration.

During this first week of proposal preparation, you have confirmed your project's appropriateness for the SBIR/STTR program. You have also completed an initial assessment of your project's strengths and weaknesses in each of the review categories and created an outline to guide your preparation. You are now ready to plunge deeper into the proposal preparation process, including the long lead-time tasks you will address in Week 2.

Time required: 15 hours

<u>Objectives</u>

This week, you will prepare an initial outline of your budget and determine which work will need to be conducted at outside institutions. You will also begin all of the tasks that require a long lead time to avoid scrambling at the last minute to pull these items together. The items that require the longest lead-time are those you will have the least control over doing yourself. These items include Letters of Support, Biographical Sketches, and quotations from subcontractors, vendors, and CROs. Additionally, you will contact appropriate NIH POs for guidance on your proposal.

<u>Tasks</u>

2.1. Prepare an initial outline of your budget, identify all work that will be done at outside institutions, and arrange for quotations and support letters.

2.2. Finalize your team of researchers and consultants, and begin preparing Biographical Sketches.

2.3. Compose your Title.

2.4. Request Letters of Support from consultants, key opinion leaders, subaward PI(s), and/or potential customers.

2.5. Contact Program Officer(s).

2.1. Prepare an initial outline of your budget, identify all work that will be done at outside institutions, and arrange for quotations and support letters.

It is helpful to prepare a rough budget early on in order to ensure that your expenses will fall within the NIH guidelines. You only need to be concerned about direct costs at this point; you can add in indirect costs and fees later. Direct costs are those that are directly attributed to your project and include salaries, supplies, consultants, and subcontracts. Your direct costs for a Phase I NIH SBIR/STTR are generally capped at approximately $150,000 (this assumes a 40% indirect rate which will be explained in more detail in Week 7) but can be higher if addressing a special topic (see below). When preparing your budget, often the most difficult rule to follow is that 67% of the budget for SBIR projects and 40% of the budget for STTR projects must be used for internal expenses of the small business (e.g., salary, material and supplies, travel, or fee-for-service work). Additionally, for STTR projects, a minimum of 30% of the budget must be directed to the partnering research institution. Consulting and subcontracts do not qualify as work being done by the small business. Therefore, for an SBIR project, you are normally allowed to spend only 33% of your total costs (approximately $83,000 for a $250,000 award) on subcontractors, subawards, and consultants. For an STTR, you have approximately $75,000 (or 30% of $250,000) to spend on outside resources, other than your partnering research institution.

>> Determine your maximum budget cap:

   □ Review the NIH SBA-Approved SBIR/STTR Topics for Awards over Statutory Budget Limitations. Each year, topics are published for each IC that has been approved for budgets exceeding the NIH budget cap. You should review the topics for ICs that are relevant to your project and determine if you feel that your project is addressing one of the listed topics.

☐ Confirm with a PO at the relevant IC if you feel that your project falls within one of the topic areas eligible for a larger budget. Budget caps for special topics generally range from $300,000 to $700,000, and you should clarify with the PO the maximum limit for your project.

☐ Your total <u>direct costs</u> will be approximately 60% of the total allowable costs. You will use the remaining allowable funds for indirect costs and fees.

>> Prepare a first draft of your budget:

☐ Read the *R&R Budget Form* section of the Application Guide, which is lengthy but very clearly written.

☐ For each Specific Aim you formulated in Week 1, list all tasks that will be necessary to complete the Aim.

☐ Prepare a budget for completing all tasks listed for each Specific Aim. First, estimate the total labor and materials costs you will incur internally. Make sure you budget sufficient salary for the PI to manage the project and that you adhere to the minimum PI time requirement of 10% effort over the project period.

☐ For STTR projects, provide your partnering institution with the cap for their budget (i.e., a minimum of 30% of the total budget). Be sure to tell your partnering institution that the provided cap is the total cost for their portion of the work (i.e., that the cap includes direct expenses in addition to their overhead costs).

☐ Estimate the total costs for work done by CROs and consultants.

☐ Ensure your budget falls within the appropriate budget guidelines. If you are substantially under the target budget, you may consider adding additional tasks and/or increasing the time commitment you allocate for personnel to complete the tasks. If you are over the target budget, you may need to cut some of the proposed work.

Once you have drafted a rough budget, you should have a clear idea of all the research tasks that will be performed during your Phase I project. You are now ready to request formal quotations from CROs and budgets from partnering institutions. It is important to request these quotes early to ensure that you receive the documents prior to submission and to ensure that you have enough money in your budget to perform all the work. Quotes can come in much higher than expected and discovering the true cost early will provide you with the time to modify your Approach if necessary. Reviewers will pay close attention to where you choose to have the work performed, so it is important to choose well-qualified CROs and partnering institutions.

>> Request quotations from all CROs, external research institutions, and all other outside groups that will perform any part of the project.

☐ Request that all quotations be provided to you at least one month before the NIH proposal submission deadline. This will give you a few weeks of buffer time to obtain a quotation from a slow CRO and/or find a new CRO if your first choice does not work out. Ask if they can provide you with a cost estimate before they send you the official quote for budgeting purposes.

□ For all <u>STTR projects</u>, you will need to request a budget from your partnering research institution. For <u>SBIR projects that include an academic collaboration</u>, you will also need to obtain a budget from the academic institution. Partnering universities will likely already be familiar with preparing budgets for NIH STTR proposals. If your partnering research institution does not have previous experience as a subawardee on STTR grants, then download the "Optional" <u>R&R Subaward Budget Attachment(s) Form 5 YR 30 ATT</u> from Grants.gov or ASSIST, and provide it to your partnering institution to complete.

>> For STTR proposals, obtain a Letter of Support from the partnering research institution.

□ A requirement of STTR proposals is for the partnering research institution to provide a letter certifying that at least 30% of the work will be performed by the research institution. The research institution will often require that a business official sign the letter, although in some cases the partnering PI may sign the letter. Read the requirements for the scope of this letter in the *PHS 398 Research Plan Form* section of the Application Guide, under the subheading *Consortium/Contractual Arrangements*.

□ Arrange for the partnering research institution to prepare the letter, and provide a clear deadline for obtaining the letter, which should usually be at least two weeks prior to the grant submission deadline. When making arrangements for this letter, be ready to provide institution officials with specifics about the application, including PI name and contact information, title of application, project period, total subaward budget amount, and solicitation number.

□ Once you receive the letter, save it as a PDF file. You will attach it to the "Consortium/Contractual Arrangements" section of the PHS 398 Research Plan form in your application in Week 9.

2.2. Finalize your team of researchers and consultants, and begin preparing Biographical Sketches.

You will need to include Biographical Sketches for all senior/key personnel. Senior/key personnel are defined as "all individuals who contribute in a substantive, meaningful way to the scientific development or execution of the project, whether or not salaries are requested." In practical terms, all skilled people working on the project, such as senior scientists, subcontractors, and consultants, should be included. You do not need to include junior scientists, technicians, interns, etc. The total number of senior/key personnel generally ranges from 3-10 for a Phase I project.

The required format for Biographical Sketches is contained in the *R&R Senior/Key Personnel Profile (Expanded) Form* section of the Application Guide. The Biographical Sketch is limited to 5 pages and includes sections for a Personal Statement, Positions and Honors, Contributions to Science, and Research Support and/or Scholastic Performance. The Personal Statement section should be customized for your proposal; make sure you take the time to write a strong Personal Statement for each individual's Biographical Sketch. You will not have space in the Research Plan to highlight the talents of each contributing team member, so you should use the Personal Statements to convey the expertise of your team. Write Personal Statements that directly pertain to the proposed project, and don't just include a generic list of the key personnel's talents. This is particularly important for consultants, as it helps to demonstrate each consultant's commitment to your project.

The Contributions to Science section allows researchers to describe up to five of their most significant contributions to science, along with the historical background that framed their research. Descriptions may include a mention of research products under development, such as manuscripts that have been submitted but have not yet been accepted for publication. Industry scientists have the opportunity to describe how their efforts contributed to the success of their current and previous companies. Many researchers find the Contributions to Science section difficult to complete, and it is tempting to gloss over this section or simply list a series of references and/or patents. However, Investigator(s) is one of the five key metrics that reviewers will use to score your application, and they will rely heavily on the Biographical Sketches during this part of their review.

>> Ask each senior/key person to prepare a first draft of his/her own Biographical Sketch. A template for the Biographical Sketch is available on the NIH website (be sure you are using the current template by checking the expiration data in the top right corner of the template). The deadline for completing this first draft should be at least one month prior to the grant submission date. Once you receive each Biographical Sketch, carefully edit the document and ensure that the Personal Statement and Contributions to Science sections highlight all areas of the individual's expertise. The Personal Statement should also clearly

state the senior/key person's role in the project and indicate how he or she is particularly qualified for this role. It may take several iterations of editing to ensure all Biographical Sketches are fully polished.

2.3. Compose your Title.

Your Title may have a maximum of 200 characters, including spaces. This Title will appear prominently throughout the review and grant period, and you will typically use the same Title for your Phase II proposal. The Title should include exactly two components: 1) the problem and 2) your solution. Examples include: "Small Molecule Inhibitors of XXX [name disease or target]"; "Diagnostic to More Rapidly Evaluate YYY"; or "Improved Sterilization Method to Reduce Food-Borne Illness".

>> Write your Title.

□ Ensure your Title achieves the two objectives of stating the problem and your solution. Count characters (including spaces) to confirm you have no more than 200.

□ You should include your Title in each of the Letters of Support that you will include with the application (see 2.4 below).

2.4. Request Letters of Support from consultants, key opinion leaders, subaward PI(s), and/or potential customers.

Letters of Support are very important to reviewers because they demonstrate external enthusiasm for your project. All consultants should provide a Letter of Support, and it is also helpful to obtain Letters of Support from key opinion leaders in the field as well as potential customers for your final product. You may also consider obtaining letters from development partners, venture capitalists, and clinicians who can vouch for both the medical need and commercial viability of your product. While Letters of Support from individuals other than consultants are not required for a Phase I application, if you are able to obtain 1-3 strong letters from potential customers or end-users, the letter(s) can enhance your proposal substantially. Additionally, if your project involves a subaward, you will need to request a Letter of Support from the subaward PI(s). You can provide the letter writers with drafts of customized letters for their convenience that they can modify.

>> Read the NIH requirements for information to be included in Letters of Support, located in the *PHS 398 Research Plan Form* section of the Application Guide.

>> Obtain signed Letters of Support from each consultant. Ensure that each letter includes the following information:

☐ The consultant's relevant background and experience as well as her/his interest in your project. The consultant should not simply commit to the project but should express enthusiasm about your technology's potential to solve a clear unmet need in the field.

☐ The total number of hours that the consultant will commit to the project and his/her hourly rate.

☐ The specific role that the consultant will serve in the project. This may include regularly scheduled phone conferences and/or onsite visits to discuss your project's progress and to obtain the consultant's expertise in a specific area.

\>\> Obtain 1-3 Letters of Support from customers, clinicians, etc., that address some or all of the following points:

☐ Background and experience of the letter writer.

☐ Enthusiasm for your technology and how it will address an unmet need.

☐ Business case for your product.

☐ Ability of your team to successfully commercialize the product.

\>\> If your project includes a subaward, it is recommended that you request a Letter of Support from your subaward PI(s). A Letter of Support from a subaward PI should include:

☐ Verification of the subaward PI's commitment to the project.

☐ Description of the subaward PI's expertise and how it is critical to the proposed project.

☐ The subaward PI's role in the project.

Request that all Letters of Support be provided to you at least one month prior to the proposal submission deadline. Once you receive the letters, scan and save them as a single PDF file.

2.5. Contact Program Officer(s).

At this point in your proposal preparation process, you probably have a number of questions! This is a great time to initiate contact with a PO to address these questions.

Additionally, it is important to confirm that the PO feels that your project is appropriate for a Phase I award before you delve into the more time-consuming aspects of preparing your proposal.

It is important not to underestimate what a fantastic resource your PO can be. Not only are POs intimately familiar with all aspects of the SBIR/STTR program, but they also have highly relevant backgrounds in several areas that can be extremely helpful to you. NIH POs usually hold doctorates in fields relevant to their ICs, and they often have extensive experience in academia, industry and/or government research positions. Many POs are very familiar with aspects of product development that you may not initially consider, such as the regulatory environment and market need. Therefore, while your initial relationship with your PO will likely involve specific questions about the SBIR/STTR program, it is in your best interest to develop a strong continuing relationship with your PO before, during, and after your award period, as your PO can be a valuable partner in helping you to successfully commercialize your product.

Given the many responsibilities of POs, they are often quite busy and may not answer their phone if you cold call them. Therefore, it is generally best to initiate contact with a PO via email to schedule a time when they will be available for a call. Also, if you introduce your proposed project via email, the PO will have time to reflect before formulating a response.

>> Include the following points in your initial email to the PO(s):

□ Introduce yourself as a first-time SBIR/STTR applicant who is seeking the PO's assistance in evaluating whether your project is a good candidate for the program.

□ Write 1-2 paragraphs about your topic and list your Specific Aims. (Keep a copy of this on file, as it will serve as a good starting point for your Project Summary.)

□ List any questions you have about the NIH SBIR/STTR program. Make sure you include any questions that arose during your self-evaluation. Be honest about what you perceive may be your proposal's weaknesses, and solicit the PO's input on how you may be able to address these weaknesses.

□ Ask the PO to confirm that your project is a good fit for the IC. Also, ask whether the SRG selection that you made in Week 1 is appropriate for your project.

□ Address the possibility of exceeding the standard budget cap if you have determined that your project falls within a special topic.

□ Request a phone call to discuss your questions about the proposal preparation process. Suggest several blocks of time when you are available for a call.

Most POs will get back to you within 48 hours and will reply favorably to your request for a phone call. Some POs prefer to communicate via email; in this case, you may need to follow up several times to get all of your questions answered. If you do not feel that you are getting the information you need from the PO whom you initially contacted, you may search the IC for other POs or you may contact POs at other ICs. You should pay very close attention to all information that your PO provides, as this will likely be the most relevant advice that you receive throughout the proposal-writing process.

If the PO feels that your project is not appropriate for the NIH SBIR/STTR program, then you should work with the PO to determine what you would need to do in order to propose a more appropriate project. If the PO indicates that your project is a good fit for the NIH SBIR/STTR program, then you are ready to move forward with the proposal preparation process!

WEEK 3

Time required: 10 hours

Objectives

This week, you will do a thorough assessment of your competition and start to lay the groundwork for differentiating your product from those of other companies. Additionally, as the use of vertebrate animals and human subjects in your project involves extra paperwork, this week you will determine whether these documents are required for your submission in order to plan for the completion of these documents in later weeks. At the end of this week, you will have completed the majority of the nuts and bolts aspects of preparing your proposal, so that you can turn your focus to the scientific writing.

Tasks

3.1. Review the competitive landscape for your product.

3.2. Assess whether you will be required to include information for Vertebrate Animals and/or Human Subjects.

3.1. Review the competitive landscape for your product.

It is very important to convince reviewers that you have a solid understanding of your competition. In Week 1 while you were doing your self-evaluation, you spent some time identifying products currently available for the unmet need you are addressing and created a list of what sets your technology apart from these products. Now it is time to do a deeper dive into the competitive landscape for your product. In doing this, you will construct a table that can serve as a reference as you gear up to write your Research Plan in Week 5.

>> Create a table with columns for the key aspects of competing products to your technology, such as company/product name, product description, stage of development, and limitations/drawbacks. Populate the table with several competing products. Be sure to include both technologies that are in development and ones that are on the market. Your table should include major players in the field in addition to any alternative strategies that are being explored as a solution to the unmet need.

The following table is an example of a summary of competitive products for a novel wound care product.

Company/ Product	Active Ingredient	Mechanism of Action	Drawbacks
Clark Stanley's / Snake Oil	Iodine	Disrupts protein and nucleic acid structure and synthesis	- Chemical instability - Toxic to host cells - No *in vivo* proof of anti-biofilm activity
Wounds R Us / Super Gel	Silver chloride	Interacts with thiol groups in enzymes and proteins to kill bacteria	- Bacterial resistance - Decreased efficacy against Gram-negative bacteria - Toxic to host cells
Antibac, Inc / Bacteria Be Gone Gel	PHMB	Interacts with negatively charged species of the membrane causing aggregation leading to increased fluidity and permeability resulting in death of the bacteria	Not effective against biofilms
Your Company / Product	**New active ingredient**	**New mechanism of action**	**- Sufficient *in vitro* support, but lacking *in vivo* demonstration of efficacy**

>> As you populate the table, review competitors' websites, publications, and patent filings to obtain up-to-date information about their technology and to assess their stage of development. If you are developing a diagnostic or a therapeutic, it is helpful to search clinicaltrials.gov to identify other products in development. Review articles may also be useful in identifying advantages and limitations of competitive technologies.

3.2. Assess whether you will be required to include information for Vertebrate Animals and/or Human Subjects.

Projects that involve the use of vertebrate animals and/or human subjects require additional documents included in the application that provide a number of details on the handling and care of animals and the safety of human subjects. The formats for the Vertebrate Animals and Human Subjects sections are well defined, but if you haven't written one of these sections before, they can be challenging and time consuming to complete. In this task, you will determine whether these documents are required for your application, familiarize yourself with the requirements, and create a plan for completing these documents.

>> Review your Specific Aims and determine if your studies will involve the use of vertebrate animals. If vertebrate animals are being sacrificed specifically for the purpose of your studies, then the answer will be yes. Sometimes studies make use of purchased animal products, such as mouse liver microsomes or rat plasma. If these are being purchased from a commercial source, then they do not qualify as vertebrate animal use. If you are unsure whether your studies qualify, then you can reach out to a PO for clarification.

>> If you determined that your project does involve the use of vertebrate animals, you are required to include a Vertebrate Animals section in the PHS 398 Research Plan form.

☐ Familiarize yourself with the required content for the Vertebrate Animals section. Skim through the Vertebrate Animals instructions in Week 7. Review these instructions to gain an understanding of the information that you need to collect. Generate a template of the Vertebrate Animals document that includes headings for the required three sections.

☐ Create a plan for completing your Vertebrate Animals section. Once you have reviewed the content to be included in this document, you should identify who can provide you with the information. If the animal work will be performed by an academic collaborator or a CRO, ask them to provide you with detailed information on the experimental design, information on the care of animals, and the method of euthanasia. You will need to inform your collaborators of the required information and provide them with a deadline for providing you with the information. If the animal studies will be conducted by your small business, then you should identify the person who will be in charge of those studies and who can provide you with the needed information.

>> Review your Specific Aims and determine if your studies will involve the use of human subjects. If humans are involved in any aspect of your research, you will need to determine which of the following NIH categories applies: 1) human subjects, but exempt from federal regulations; 2) use of human subjects, not exempt; or 3) clinical trial. If you need help determining whether your application includes human subjects, review the instructions in the *R&R Other Project Information Form* section of the Application Guide and take advantage of the questionnaire that is referenced in the instructions. Some use of human subjects falls under exemptions that then lessen the document requirements for the application. NIH provides an "Exempt Human Subjects Research Infographic" that summarizes a total of 8 exemptions with basic definitions and examples. Because NIH does not require Institutional Review Board (IRB) approval at the time of application, the exemptions designated often represent the opinion of the PI, and the justification provided for the exemption by the PI is evaluated during peer review. If you are still unclear on the designation of your research after reviewing the instructions and infographic, be sure to talk to a PO for further clarification. Once you feel confident in your answer regarding the use of human subjects, you will then need to review the required documentation for human subjects and create a plan for completing these documents.

☐ Familiarize yourself with the required content for the Human Subjects section. Detailed instructions for completing this section are found in Week 7. Review these instructions to gain an understanding of the information that you need to collect. We recommend that you generate a checklist of the required information that applies to your specific protocol.

☐ Create a plan for completing your Human Subjects section. If the human subjects studies will be performed outside of your company, you will need to request the necessary information from your academic collaborator or CRO. You should notify these parties of the information needed and set a deadline for them to provide you with the requested information. If your company will be executing the human subjects work independently then you will need to identify a person to be responsible for gathering the required information.

During this week, you have taken initial steps toward objectively evaluating the competition and clearly identifying aspects of your technology that provide you with unique advantages in addressing the unmet need. In addition, you have determined whether your project involves vertebrate animals or human subjects research, which requires additional documentation for your proposal submission. You are now ready to conduct a careful review of the literature to support the premise of your proposed research.

WEEK 4
Time required: 15 hours

<u>Objectives</u>

You have spent three weeks focusing predominantly on the administrative and long lead-time aspects of your proposal. Now it is time to spend a few weeks concentrating on the science, which for us scientists is generally the most fun part of writing a proposal! Even though you likely already have an excellent understanding of your scientific field, it is critical to be up to date on the latest research to help build the case for your innovative approach. It is also important that you cite references throughout your proposal to demonstrate to reviewers that there is literature to support your statements. A strong Phase I proposal will generally contain between 30 and 100 references. Given the importance of including references in your proposal and the time-consuming nature of finding references, you will spend the majority of your time this week researching relevant literature. You will also ensure that you have addressed the useful information that you received from the PO during your call.

<u>Tasks</u>

4.1. Identify references to include in your Significance and Innovation sections.

4.2. Identify references to include in your Approach section.

4.3. Complete follow-ups from conversations with PO(s).

4.1. Identify references to include in your Significance and Innovation sections.

In Week 1, you outlined the key points of your Significance and Innovation sections during your "self-evaluation" and in formulating your outline. You should now find literature references to support each one of these key points. In general, it is best to cite literature that is as recent as possible and from major journals. If you don't have access to an online library, most colleges and universities (especially public institutions) will allow you to use their search engines and obtain articles as long as you are physically in the library. So, if you have not been to a library in a while, this is a good time to pay one a visit! If you have access to Endnote or other reference management software, it will be helpful to create your reference library using that software. If you do not have access to reference management software, you will need to type in each reference by hand when you write your proposal.

>> Identify, read, and sort references that will be used to support your project's Significance and Innovation sections.

□ Retrieve the outline you created in Week 1 and update it as needed. This will serve as a guide as you begin to identify key references for the Significance and Innovation sections.

□ Identify references that address the severity of the unmet need. Sort data into categories of health impact (e.g., # of deaths per year), economic impact (e.g., cost to hospitals), and social impact (e.g., reduction in quality of life.) Make sure you collect information in all three of these categories and prioritize quantitative data over blanket statements. For example, it is a much stronger point to say a disease impacts

100,000 people each year in the US than that a disease impacts "a lot" of people.

☐ Identify references that discuss current state-of-the-art technologies. For each currently available option, make note of the strengths and limitations of that option. Keep track of ways in which your technology will address some or all of the limitations of current market-leading products.

☐ Identify references that address market conditions. While you will not need to write extensively about product commercialization in your Phase I proposal, you should provide a high-level overview of your market size, barriers to market entry, and how you plan to address these barriers.

☐ Identify references that support your scientific premise and the rigor of the prior research. Your Significance section will include a paragraph that summarizes the science that serves as the foundation for your project and evaluates the strengths and weaknesses of this previous work. Identify the key sources that inform your proposed work, and be prepared to provide an assessment of the rigor of those studies.

4.2. Identify references to include in your Approach section.

When you begin writing your Research Strategy, you will quickly find how difficult it is to fit the Significance, Innovation, and Approach sections into six pages. One of the most efficient ways to save space is to reference protocols wherever possible in your Approach section, rather than writing them out explicitly. Literature references will provide reviewers with the confidence that you can successfully execute the proposed studies.

>> Refer once again to the outline you created in Week 1 and the list of all tasks required to complete each Specific Aim that you created in Week 2. Review these documents for completeness and modify as needed.

□ For each task, identify the protocols that you will employ that are based on literature precedent. Obtain references for each of these protocols.

□ If you will be proposing any experimental procedures for which you will be developing new techniques, obtain references on related protocols to support the feasibility and scientific validity of your new procedure(s). In general, the more innovative your procedure, the more evidence you should cite to support your proposed work.

4.3. Complete follow-ups from conversations with PO(s).

By now, you should have had a chance to discuss your technology and your proposed project with one or more POs. While making a valuable connection is one reason for having these calls, another reason is so you can obtain feedback on your project. We highly recommend that you carefully listen to the POs' advice and <u>address all of the POs' suggestions</u>.

>> Address all suggestions that you receive during your calls with POs. PO recommendations often include:

□ Further clarification of your end product.

□ Filling a gap in team expertise.

☐ Proposing a scope of work appropriate for a Phase I proposal.

☐ Additional tips to help you prepare a more competitive application.

At the end of this week, you should have several dozen references that are ready to insert as you begin writing your Research Plan. You have also addressed feedback from your PO in order to take advantage of this expert assessment of your project's fit for a Phase I SBIR/STTR grant.

This week, you will begin writing your Research Plan, starting with the Significance and Innovation sections. You will also follow up on outstanding requests for quotations, Biographical Sketches, and Letters of Support to ensure that these long lead-time items are on track to meet the submission deadline.

Tasks

5.1. Prepare to write your Research Plan.

5.2. Write the Significance section of your Research Strategy.

5.3. Write the Innovation section of your Research Strategy.

5.4. Follow up on quotations, Biographical Sketches, and Letters of Support.

5.1. Prepare to write your Research Plan.

The heart of your SBIR/STTR application is your seven-page Research Plan. Three of the five review criteria categories are directly addressed in the Research Plan: Significance, Innovation, and Approach. As indicated in the diagram below, the Research Plan consists of a one-page introduction called your Specific Aims page and then six pages devoted to your Research Strategy. Your Research Strategy incorporates a Significance section, an Innovation section, and an Approach section. This week, you will focus on the Significance and Innovation sections, and next week you will write the Approach section and prepare your Specific Aims page.

RESEARCH PLAN

	Specific Aims page (1 page)	
Research Strategy (6 pages)	Significance (½ – 1 page)	
	Innovation (½ – 1 page)	
	Approach (4-5 pages)	

>> Create a document for your Research Plan, using MS Word or a similar program. Your Research Plan will initially be saved as a single file. When it is time to upload it to your application, you will need to subdivide it into separate files (see Week 8).

□ Open a new document and save it as "Research Plan". Add section headers for Specific Aims, Significance, Innovation, Approach, and References.

□ There are specific requirements for font selection, font size, and page margins set by the NIH, which can be accessed by selecting the "Format Attachments" hyperlink located in the *Application Process* section of the Application Guide, under the subheading *Write Application*. We have found that 11-point Arial works well to maximize the number of words that fit on a page, and NIH allows 0.5-inch margins on all sides. Note that you may use a smaller font size for figures and graphs, which can save some space. Do not include page numbers or any other text in the headers or footers, as this will overlap with text inserted by the submission system when it generates the assembled application.

□ Insert a page break after the Specific Aims page, since this section is limited to 1 page. The reason you should not save the Specific Aims page as a separate file at this time is that you will want to have consistent sequential reference endnotes for both the Specific Aims page and for the Research Strategy.

□ Ideally, you should load the references you identified in Week 4 into a reference management program. Endnote is a popular choice, and there are also several free options available on the Internet. If you do not have a reference management program, then you will need to insert references manually as you prepare your Research Plan.

5.2. Write the Significance section of your Research Strategy.

The goal of the Significance section of the Research Strategy is to describe the <u>unmet need</u> you will be addressing and to convey <u>how your technology will provide a solution for this unmet need</u>. The importance of the Significance section cannot be over-emphasized. If you do not provide a convincing argument for the significance of your product, all of the effort you put into the other sections of your proposal will be irrelevant. If your product does not address a clearly stated, critical unmet need, there is no reason for the government to invest money in your project.

Some proposal writers are understandably confused about the difference between the Significance and Innovation sections. While there can be some overlap between these sections, you should use the Significance section to focus on how your technology will alleviate an unmet need and save the details about the novelty of your approach for the Innovation section. For example, the Significance section may state that your technology, if successfully developed, will save 10,000 lives each year, while the Innovation section may detail how your technology solves the problem in a unique manner.

You should aim for approximately ¾ of a page for your Significance section, although a length between ½ and 1 page is reasonable. You already have all the information you need to complete the Significance section from your research in Week 4. Now, you should spend some time on your <u>clarity of presentation</u>, so that you can effectively convey the significance of your technology to reviewers.

Tips for clarity of presentation:

1. <u>The "five sentence" approach to writing a paragraph</u>, which you may have learned in elementary school, is a fantastic tool for effectively making a convincing argument that is well-supported by facts. In a "five sentence" paragraph, the first sentence provides a statement of purpose. The subsequent three sentences support the statement with detailed, independent facts. The final sentence concludes and strengthens the initial statement. Here are some examples of effective "five sentence" paragraphs:

Example #1. There is a clear unmet need for better treatments for XYZ Disease. Over 100,000 patients are affected by the disease each year in the US, and current treatment options are only 50% effective (ref 1). XYZ Disease is especially prevalent in children, and 50% of all cases are diagnosed in individuals under 18 years old (ref 2). The incidence of this disease is rapidly increasing, and the disease is projected to afflict 130,000 people in the US annually by 2025 (ref 3). There is clearly a need for better therapeutics to treat this devastating disease.

Example #2. Current state-of-the-art diagnostics for PQR Disease are insufficient for correct diagnosis. The most common diagnostic assay is the ABC assay, which has a documented false negative readout in 40% of cases (ref 1). Other assays under development rely on the DEF technology, and even under optimal circumstances, the incidence of false negative readouts is predicted to be 20% when DEF technology is employed (ref 2). Patients who receive false negative diagnoses do not receive the immediate care that is necessary to prevent long-term suffering from the illness, and 20% of cases that are not immediately treated result in mortality (ref 3). Given the serious consequences of PQR Disease, it is important to develop a diagnostic that approaches 100% accuracy.

Each of the above examples provides a convincing argument for an <u>unmet need</u> and includes quantitative statements that convey the severity of the problem. In Example #2, the writer focuses not only on the limitations of current technologies but also on the limitations of competitive technologies under development, which is an excellent strategy to convince reviewers to fund your technology over another potential technology.

2. <u>Use references liberally</u>. It is important to reference all statements of fact, and it is preferable to include multiple references for each point, particularly if your statement may be

considered controversial. The best references are those from highly regarded peer reviewed journals in your field. Non-peer reviewed citations such as "personal communication" are generally weak, and website references should be avoided unless you are referencing a well-established source, such as the NIH website. Do not include Wikipedia articles as references, but you may find the links that are available in Wikipedia or similar sites useful in tracking down relevant primary references.

3. <u>Use correct grammar</u>. While this point should go without saying, a surprising number of proposals are submitted with poor grammar. Poor grammar reduces the professionalism of your proposal and can interfere with the ability of reviewers to understand and appreciate your proposed work. If you are not a native English speaker, or if you have trouble with grammar, it is particularly important to have your proposal proof-read. If you don't have ready access to a colleague with strong English skills, it is well worth the expense of having a professional edit your proposal.

4. <u>Use headings, figures, and formatting to emphasize key points</u>. Keep in mind that reviewers will be reading many other proposals in addition to yours. Make their job as easy as possible by highlighting key information with headings, figures, and formatting. It is also helpful to use bolding or underlining to emphasize key phrases or sentences, such as the unmet need your product will address, or how your product will address that need.

>> Write your Significance section.

□ Read the information provided under the *Research Strategy* subheading in the *PHS 398 Research Plan form* section of the

Application Guide, which provides an overview of the proposal components you will be writing over the next several weeks. Carefully review the instructions for the Significance section. The Application Guide outlines several points that should be discussed, including the unmet need that your technology will address and the rigor of the prior research that serves as key support for your project.

□ Write your opening paragraph, based loosely on the "five sentence" paragraph format described above. Your first sentence should clearly state the problem (e.g., the impact of the disease you are addressing or inadequacies in current systems that you will be solving). Include supporting sentences that focus on the health-related aspects of the problem, but also address economic and societal factors. Conclude this paragraph by reemphasizing the need for a better solution.

□ Write 1-2 additional paragraphs to further describe the unmet need that your technology will address. There may be specific issues that need further clarification, such as the pathogenesis of the disease you are addressing or the limitations of current products. Remember that the reviewers may not be experts in your field, so you should educate them on specific technical issues that are limiting current products on the market and others in development.

□ The next paragraph should introduce your technology, and it should specify the ways your technology will address the unmet need. Be as specific as possible about the problem you are solving and the impact your solution will have on all aspects of the problem (health, economic, and societal).

◻ The final paragraph will address the Rigor of Prior Research, and we recommend that you include a sub-heading, "Rigor of Prior Research", to help reviewers easily identify this section. This assessment of rigor will state the general experimental rigor of the studies that have been done that support the premise of your proposed project in addition to identifying gaps in the research and plans to address these gaps. For example, you can support your approach to treating a disease by summarizing the relevant clinical studies that have been published and indicate if these studies had sufficient power due to group sizes, use of proper controls, and/or population diversity. If the rigor of the prior research is poor, discuss how your technology will enable more rigorous study moving forward. For instance, there may be no easy way to identify effective treatments for disease X because each clinical trial used a different approach for diagnosing the disease. Development of your diagnostic will enable the comparison of trial results by identifying patients early and ensuring that consistent diagnostic criteria are applied to all participants.

◻ Once you have finished writing your Significance section, re-read the instructions in the Application Guide to ensure you have addressed all points that are listed. Then, refer to the "Application Review Information" section of your FOA. Here, you will find a summary of the Scored Review Criteria used by NIH to evaluate your application. Read the questions listed under the "Significance" header in the FOA. Evaluate your Significance section from the point of view of the reviewer, and make sure it addresses all of the questions the reviewers will use to evaluate the significance of your proposal.

Although your Significance section is only a few paragraphs in length, it must convey to reviewers that you are addressing a real and serious problem. The stronger you position the unmet need in your Significance section, the better you will set up your subsequent Innovation section.

5.3. Write the Innovation section of your Research Strategy.

Your proposal's innovation is <u>the main factor</u> on which the funding decision will be based. In fact, your project's innovation is so important that the "I" in SBIR stands for "Innovation". In Week 1, you performed a self-assessment and in Week 2, you communicated with your PO to ensure your project was sufficiently innovative to be considered for an SBIR award. Now, you must eloquently convince reviewers of the innovative nature of your technology. The Innovation section should be similar in length to the Significance section, in the range of ½ to 1 page long.

There are several synonyms of "innovation" that you may want to use as you write your Innovation section to avoid overuse of the word "innovation". These include: paradigm-changing, unique, groundbreaking, new direction, original, inventive, cutting-edge, novel, state-of-the-art, etc. Don't be afraid to use one or more of these strong words or phrases to convey the innovation of your technology, but make sure you always provide powerful facts to back up your statements.

>> Prepare to write your Innovation Section.

☐ Read the "Innovation" instructions in the *PHS 398 Research Plan Form* section of the Application Guide, under the subheading *Research Strategy*. The guide provides several suggestions that will assist you in highlighting the uniqueness of your approach.

□ Create a table with two columns as a tool to help you organize the material you will include in this section. In the left column, make a list of all innovative aspects of your technology. Then, in the right column, list the outcomes (health, economic, societal) that may be directly attributed to each innovation. If any one of your innovations does not have a direct beneficial outcome that can be linked to it, cross it out, as this will become a red herring for reviewers. An example of an innovation table for a proposal about a novel software system for physicians is provided below:

Innovation	Outcome
Software allows physicians to easily enter patient data rather than writing information by hand.	Doctor error is reduced (predict the amount by which error will be reduced; include literature citations.)
Software is less expensive than current options.	Physicians will be more likely to invest in your product. (Include data or Letters of Support on physicians' tolerance for the cost of software.)
Software is faster than other options.	Doctors can see more patients in a given time or devote more attention to patients.

Your table may have one significant innovation with several benefits, or there may be several different innovations. Either way is fine, and this will dictate how you approach writing your Innovation section. In the first case, you will focus most of your writing on the many outcomes of the single key innovation; in the second case, you will highlight all of the innovative ideas that are incorporated into your product.

>> Write your Innovation section, again using the "five sentence" approach to aid in constructing well-supported paragraphs.

□ Your opening paragraph should restate the unmet need, which should tie in nicely with your Significance section, and stress how your technology will address this unmet need. Your goal is to convince reviewers that your technology overcomes existing limitations, and that it is better than any other existing or potential solution to the problem.

□ Write 2-3 supporting paragraphs that provide more detail around the innovative aspects of your technology. Mention any patents that you have filed, as well as plans to file additional patents.

□ Define your final product. One of the review criteria is "commercial potential", so reviewers need enough information about your product to evaluate whether it will be commercially viable. Although the details of your final product may change during the course of development, you should provide sufficient information here to demonstrate that you have thought through a clear pathway to commercialization. If there will be any hurdles to commercialization, such as cost of goods or market adoption, you should state them here and define how you will overcome them.

□ It can be useful to include a comparison chart with bullet points on the capabilities of current technologies and the differential advantages of your technology. You can use the table that you created in Week 3 or a variation of it. While this type of illustration is not required, it is a great way to emphasize key points and ensure that reviewers clearly understand the benefit of your technology/approach.

□ Your conclusion paragraph should emphasize the groundbreaking nature of your product and explicitly convey the impact your product will have on improving health outcomes.

□ Once you have finished writing your Innovation section, re-read the instructions for the Innovation section in the Application Guide to ensure you have addressed all points that are listed. As you did for the Significance section, refer to the Scored Review Criteria listed in the "Application Review Information" section of the FOA. Read the questions listed under the "Innovation" header and assess your Innovation section from the point of view of a reviewer. Make sure your section addresses all the questions the reviewers will use to evaluate the innovation of your proposal.

5.4. Follow up on quotations, Biographical Sketches, and Letters of Support.

It has now been three weeks since you initiated requests for quotations, Biographical Sketches, and Letters of Support. This week, make a list of outstanding items and reach out to those who are responsible for providing the documents. Remind these individuals of the deadline for providing you with these document(s), which should be at least 1 month prior to the proposal submission due date. Make sure you stay on top of these long lead-time items as you continue to focus on your proposal writing in the subsequent weeks.

WEEK 6
Time required: 25 hours

Objectives

You will spend most of this week writing the Approach section of your Research Strategy, which details your technical plan for conducting your proposed project. Your challenge will be to include as much information as you can in a concise 4-5 page section. Once you have completed your Approach, you will write your final Specific Aims page that introduces your Research Strategy. Finally, you will initiate your application in ASSIST and will begin populating the forms.

Tasks

6.1. Write the Approach section of your Research Strategy.

6.2. Write the final Specific Aims page of your Research Plan.

6.3. Familiarize yourself with ASSIST and fill out the administrative sections of the application.

6.1. Write the Approach section of your Research Strategy.

The Approach section of your Research Strategy will likely receive the majority of the critiques by reviewers. If you are an academic investigator or have experience writing research proposals, you are at a significant advantage. If you do not have this experience, it is strongly recommended that you work with a collaborator or grant consultant to help guide you through writing your first Approach section. This section must be constructed strategically to convince reviewers that you are able to carry out a hypothesis-driven research project to advance your technology.

As described in Week 5, your Research Strategy is limited to 6 pages and consists of the Significance, Innovation, and Approach sections. Since you have already written your Significance and Innovation sections, you know how much space remains for your Approach section. There are several methods for constructing an Approach section, and the key is to be organized, logical, and concise. For each experiment you propose, you need to define clear metrics of success that you will use to determine whether your Phase I SBIR/STTR project should be advanced to a Phase II SBIR/STTR project. You also should propose alternative experiments in case your initial approach is unsuccessful. You should provide enough detail to convince reviewers of your competence, but don't be too wordy, or you will run out of space.

>> Write your Approach section.

☐ Read the instructions for completing the Approach section, found in the *PHS 398 Research Plan Form* section of the Application Guide, under the subheading *Research Strategy*.

◻ Begin with an introductory paragraph to provide an overview of the project and highlight the team. This should serve as a transition from the Significance and Innovation sections, which highlight <u>why</u> your work should be funded, to the Approach section, which addresses <u>how</u> you will complete the proposed project. You should broadly outline the technical goals of your project and how they will advance the development of your product. It is also helpful to introduce your team and consultants here, especially if you can point to some highly experienced individuals with the expertise to conduct the proposed project.

◻ If you have preliminary data, incorporate it into approximately ¾ of a page. Sufficient detail regarding the design and execution of preliminary studies is needed so reviewers can assess the rigor of these supporting studies. If the studies have been published, less detail can be provided in the Approach section as you can reference the publication for additional details. Include only conclusive, robust data that are critical for your current project, and that serves to de-risk the experiments you are proposing in your Specific Aims.

◻ Include information on "Rigor & Reproducibility", which is a relatively new requirement for NIH proposals. In this section, you should explain how your experimental design and methods will lead to robust and unbiased results. This includes describing the rationale behind using particular strains/species; how you will analyze your data; and the reasoning behind each experiment's n (e.g., providing a power analysis). It may be more efficient in terms of space to include a summary paragraph near the beginning or at the end of the Approach section that details your Rigor & Reproducibility plans for all Aims. Alternatively, it may be more sensible to discuss Rigor & Reproducibility separately in the context of each Aim. Although you may notice some content overlap between Rigor & Reproducibility and the Vertebrate Animals and Authentication of Key Resources sections, make sure you explicitly include a discussion of Rigor & Reproducibility in your Approach section.

☐ Write a separate section for each Specific Aim. If possible, break down each Aim into two or three Subaims.

☐ For each Aim/Subaim, state the purpose or rationale of the experiment(s) and the methodology you will employ. Include this information under the subheadings of "Rationale" and "Experimental Methods". You should heavily reference all aspects of your experimental protocol that are based on literature precedent. If you are proposing new methodologies, you should provide a convincing argument for their scientific validity and technical feasibility.

☐ Detail the statistical analysis you will employ. Make a strong case to support your chosen sample size, number of replicates, etc. Reviewers tend to focus heavily on the statistical aspects of your proposal to ensure you generate scientifically rigorous data. If your team does not have a strong background in statistics, you should identify a consultant with this expertise to include on your team.

☐ At the end of each Aim/Subaim, include a separate paragraph with an underlined or italicized header labeled "Metrics of Success" or "Milestones". Define one or more metrics that must be achieved in order for the Aim to be considered successful and to warrant further development of your technology. Your metrics should be measurable and quantitative. For example, a metric should not be "improved efficacy". A more appropriate metric would be "a ten percent decrease in tumor growth compared to the control".

☐ For each Aim/Subaim, include a separate section that describes "Expected Results and Alternative Approaches". Brainstorm everything that could go wrong with your study and provide at least one, and preferably two alternative plans. It is important that you do not try to hide a weakness or uncertainty in your experimental design from the reviewers. They will identify all high-risk aspects of your plan and will penalize you if you do not address them with potential alternative experiments. It is best if you can construct your first Aim to be relatively low-risk and save your higher-risk experiments for later Aims. That way, reviewers will be comfortable that your project won't fail early on, which would result in a waste of the remaining funds.

☐ At either the beginning or end of the Approach section, it is helpful to include a timeline, which may be presented in the form of a Gantt chart, so reviewers can visualize how you plan to schedule your experiments throughout the grant period. Make sure you add about 30% to the time you think each Specific Aim will require to allow for unforeseen delays. Reviewers tend to favor proposals with a less ambitious timeline because there is a greater likelihood that the project will be successfully completed. Also, when you submit your Phase II proposal, it is much better to state that you exceeded your Phase I expectations than that your project was incomplete.

☐ The conclusion to your Approach section is your last chance to convince reviewers that they should fund your proposal.

Your conclusion paragraph should restate your strongest argument(s) for why your proposal should be funded. It should also clearly indicate the milestones that will be achieved during the proposed Phase I project and how these milestones will advance your product development. It is helpful to allude to your Phase II project and how your Phase I work will justify and de-risk the larger investments that will be made in Phase II and beyond.

□ Once you have finished writing your Approach section, re-read the instructions for the Approach section in the Application Guide to ensure you have addressed all points that are listed. Then, refer to the Scored Review Criteria in the FOA, listed in the "Application Review Information" section. Read the questions listed under the "Approach" header. Assess your Approach section from the point of view of the reviewer, and make sure it addresses all of the questions the reviewer will use to evaluate your proposal.

>> Review your entire Research Plan, including the Significance, Innovation, and Approach sections, to ensure that they flow together well and that they provide a compelling argument for funding your proposed work. The **Appendix** of this book contains a checklist of key items that you should make sure you have included in your Research Strategy.

6.2. Write the final Specific Aims page of your Research Plan.

The Specific Aims page serves as a one-page introduction to your Research Strategy. You should use this page to introduce your proposal and highlight key points of your technology. The Specific Aims page is one of the most important pages in your application and may be the only section that many of the reviewers read. You should write a very engaging Specific Aims page to motivate reviewers to read further. You do not have room to include many details on this page. This can be used to your advantage in that you can provide tantalizing snippets about your project that will be further developed in your Research Strategy. Use the Specific Aims information you pulled together in Week 1 as you were conducting your self-assessment as a starting point and round out this information with the components discussed below.

>> Write your Specific Aims page.

□ Read the instructions for completing the Specific Aims page in the *PHS 398 Research Plan Form* section of the Application Guide, under the subheading *Specific Aims*.

□ Write 1-2 paragraphs that introduce the unmet need and how your technology will address this need. You should draw on the concepts included in your Significance and Innovation sections, but the Specific Aims page should be written at a higher level, with much less detail. These paragraphs should be composed with the explicit goal of engaging the reviewer and convincing her/him of the importance of your work. Make sure to provide a clear picture of your end product.

□ Write 1 paragraph describing the scope of your Phase I project. Include a brief summary of preliminary efforts that support the proposed project. Introduce your planned research and the milestones you expect to achieve. End this paragraph with a phrase such as, "To this end, the Specific Aims of our Phase I project are:"

☐ List each of your Specific Aims, starting each Aim on a new line. After each aim, write 1-3 sentences about the rationale, how it will be accomplished, the expected outcome, and your metric for success.

☐ Conclude your Specific Aims page with a statement about the ultimate goal of the proposed project to remind reviewers of the relevance of your proposal. For example, you may start your final sentence with, "If successful, this Phase I project will result in…"

6.3. Familiarize yourself with ASSIST and fill out administrative sections of the application.

To make the online submission process easier, it is important to familiarize yourself with NIH ASSIST, the web-based portal you will use to prepare and submit your grant application. ASSIST provides a relatively intuitive graphical interface through which you will enter administrative information, upload your grant documents, and submit your application. In our experience, working with ASSIST is most easily learned through hands-on experience, and we recommend that you simply log in to ASSIST and explore the system rather than reading the detailed ASSIST User Guide. Of course, the User Guide can be referenced as needed if you run into any problems.

>> Locate the ASSIST portal on the web and log in using your company's eRA Commons SO account. On the home screen, you will see an "INITIATE APPLICATION" option in the center menu, and to the right, under "Resources" you will see links to the Application Guide and the ASSIST User Guide. In the box next to "INITIATE APPLICATION," enter the FOA number from the FOA that you identified in Week 1. (Make sure you use the

correct opportunity number!) Press "Go", and you will be prompted to provide an Application Project Title – enter the Title that you composed in Week 2. You also have the option of specifying the PI for your proposal. A button will allow you to pre-fill your PI's information by entering his/her eRA Commons username. If you enter a PI at this time, this individual's information will automatically be populated to other forms within the application. (If necessary, the PI information can be changed manually later.) Click the "Initiate Application" button.

>> After you initiate your application, navigate through the other tabs to familiarize yourself with the format. Click on each one of the ASSIST subsection tabs and read through the questions and required documents. Each tab corresponds to a separate form that will be associated with your application. It may also be useful to have your Application Guide handy to help walk you through the process of filling out the application. By taking the time to practice using ASSIST and referencing the Application Guide and the Annotated Form Set as needed, you will minimize unexpected surprises when it is time to submit your application.

>> Add necessary optional forms by selecting "ADD OPTIONAL FORM" in the left-hand menu. Once you select "ADD OPTIONAL FORM", there will be a new window with a dropdown list. Click the arrow of the dropdown list and you will see a menu with the available optional forms. If your proposal includes a subaward and you are submitting an SBIR, you will need to add the R&R Subaward Budget form (If you are submitting an STTR application, the R&R Subaward Budget form will already be a tab within your application and will not need to be added as an optional form). Although the PHS Assignment Request form is also listed as optional, it is to your advantage to complete this as well.

>> In the *Application Process* section of the Application Guide, locate the "Obtain Software" link under the *Prepare to Apply and Register* subheading. Click this link and ensure that you have all of the necessary software you will need for submitting your proposal.

>> Carefully read all formatting instructions for your proposal. In the *Application Process* section of the Application Guide, under the *Write Application* subheading, click the "Format Attachments" link to view this information. The NIH has very specific guidance on formatting your proposal, including text, spacing, and file name requirements. It is important that you follow all guidelines, or your proposal may be rejected. It is helpful to bookmark these instructions so that you can return to them once you begin writing.

>> Fill out the following administrative sections of the application. Save your work in the application often so that you don't lose the information that you have entered. To save the information and keep a form open for further editing, click the "Save and Keep Lock" button. To save the information and close the form, click the "Save and Release Lock" button. As it is likely that you will need to come back and enter information at a later time as you are populating the different sections of the application, we recommend that you maintain a list of required items that are outstanding as you move through the tabs of the application in ASSIST.

☐ Click on the "R&R Cover" tab and click "Edit". Complete the majority of the SF 424 (R&R) form, following the guidelines in the *SF 424 (R&R) Form* section of the Application Guide. Note any items that you are unable to complete, so that you can finish them once you have the necessary information.

□ Click the "Cover Page Supplement" tab and complete the PHS 398 Cover Page Supplement form, following the guidelines in the *PHS 398 Cover Page Supplement Form* section of the Application Guide. This form is straightforward.

□ Click on the "Other Project Information" tab and complete portions of the Research & Related Other Project Information form, following the guidelines in the *R&R Other Project Information Form* section of the Application Guide. Fill in only the administrative portions of this form. You will populate the Vertebrate Animals and Human Subjects questions in Week 7 and will upload the Project Summary/Abstract, Project Narrative, Bibliography & References Cited, Facilities & Other Resources, and Equipment documents later when the documents are complete.

□ Click on the "Sites" tab, and complete the Project/Performance Site Location(s) form, following the guidelines in the *Project/Performance Site Location(s) Form* section of the Application Guide. You will need to provide the location where the work will be completed. The primary location should be your company's facility, and the address should match the one you used to obtain your DUNS number. Other Project/Performance Site Locations should include the partnering research institution for STTR applicants as well as any institution(s) where a significant portion of the project will be conducted for both STTR and SBIR applicants.

□ Click the "Sr/Key Person Profile" tab and complete the Research & Related Senior/Key Person Profile (Expanded) form, following the guidelines in the *R&R Senior/Key Person Profile (Expanded) Form* section of the Application Guide. Fill out the required information for each senior/key person. Be sure to supply the organization for all personnel; although this is not listed as a "required" field, your application will have an error if this information is not supplied. Next, attach all Biographical Sketches that have been completed. Remember to attach the Biographical Sketches as PDF files. <u>Be sure to insert your PI's eRA Commons ID in the "Credential, e.g., agency login" box, as your application cannot be processed unless you include this information.</u> Note that you do <u>not</u> need to include any information in the "Current & Pending Support" field.

□ Click the "SBIR/STTR Information" tab and complete the <u>SBIR/STTR Information</u> form, following the guidelines in the *SBIR/STTR Information Form* section of the Application Guide. On this form, you will provide the SBC Control ID you were given when you completed your SBA registration. Note that you must select either SBIR or STTR, and you may not select "both." Make sure that your selection in this section matches the FOA you entered when initiating your application (i.e., either SBIR or STTR). We strongly recommend arranging to complete all research in the United States. If you propose to have work done in a foreign country and NIH does not accept your justification for why this is necessary, you may be required to find a US site to perform the studies before the NIH will grant the award, even if it is more cost effective to perform the studies abroad. You do <u>not</u> include a Commercialization Plan for Phase I.

>> When you are ready to access your application again to add finalized components, you will log in to ASSIST and choose "Search Applications" from the Home menu. Search "Work in Progress" to locate the application that you initiated this week. Select that application, and you will be directed to the

"Summary" tab. You can then select the appropriate tab to complete additional sections of the application.

This has been a busy week! You have now completed your Research Plan, which will be the most critically reviewed section of your proposal. You should reread each section in your Research Plan several times in the subsequent weeks to ensure that you have conveyed all the information you feel will be relevant to convince reviewers of the value of your project. You have also initiated your application in ASSIST, and you will continue to populate this application in the upcoming weeks as you finalize documents for the submission.

<u>Objectives</u>

Your main goal this week is to seek as much constructive feedback as you can on your Research Plan. While you are waiting for your plan to be reviewed, you should ensure all quotations, Letters of Support, and Biographical Sketches have been completed. You will also complete your Facilities & Other Resources and Equipment sections and prepare your Budget. If your project requires the Vertebrate Animals, Human Subjects, Authentication of Key Resources, Select Agents, Resource Sharing Plan, and/or Multiple PD/PI Leadership Plan, you should complete them this week.

<u>Tasks</u>

7.1. Solicit at least two independent reviews of your proposal.

7.2. Confirm that you have received all materials requested from external sources.

7.3. Write your Facilities & Other Resources and Equipment sections.

7.4. Prepare your Budget.

7.5. Complete each of the following sections as needed for your proposal: Vertebrate Animals, Human Subjects, Authentication of Key Resources, Select Agents, Resource Sharing Plan, and Multiple PD/PI Leadership Plan.

7.1. Solicit at least two independent reviews of your proposal.

External reviewers are extremely valuable in identifying weak areas of your proposal that need more work. It is particularly important to choose appropriate reviewers who have a strong understanding of how SBIR/STTR proposals should be written. Most states have a small business resource center with a staff member on hand who will review proposals for free or for a small cost. Individuals who have previously received SBIR/STTR awards are also a good choice for reviewing your proposal. In addition, we highly recommend obtaining an independent review from a grant consultant with expertise in reviewing SBIR/STTR proposals. An external review by an experienced grant consultant may make the difference between being awarded $250,000 or not receiving the award, so the money is well spent if you can afford it. Additionally, some states will reimburse either all or a portion of the expenses paid to external consultants when preparing an SBIR/STTR proposal.

>> Identify a minimum of 2 reviewers and send them your Research Plan to review. Ask your reviewers to evaluate your proposal as if they were on your SRG, and ask them to answer the following questions:

□ What are the most convincing arguments for the significance of this work? What are ways that I can make these arguments stronger?

□ In what ways is the proposed technology innovative? What ideas do you have for strengthening the Innovation section?

□ Are there any aspects of the Research Plan, especially the Approach, that are unclear?

□ Have I appropriately described all aspects of the research and justified why the research is relevant to advancing development of the product? If not, what suggestions do you have for improving the Approach section?

□ Have I adequately detailed the statistical analyses I will use to evaluate my data?

□ Have I clearly delineated go/no-go parameters?

□ Are there any aspects of my experimental design, particularly any high-risk experiments, that do not have adequate back-up plans?

□ What ideas do you have for organizing the proposal in a way that would be easier for reviewers to understand?

□ Is the grammar correct, and are the style and tone of the writing appropriate for an SBIR/STTR proposal?

>> Ask your reviewers to provide their critiques on your 7-page Research Plan within one week, so that you have sufficient time to address their comments. Schedule a time for a follow-up meeting or teleconference so that you have an opportunity to discuss their feedback.

7.2. Confirm that you have received all materials requested from external sources.

You are now within one month of the proposal submission due date, so you will want to ensure that you have received all materials that rely on external sources, including quotations, Letters of Support, and Biographical Sketches. It is common for a vendor to fall through or another unexpected mishap to occur. Perhaps a quotation came in substantially over-budget or a consultant changed his/her mind about working on the project. If this is the case, remember to stay calm as this is a common scenario and you have purposely given yourself a month of breathing room to address any issues.

>> Assemble all quotations, Letters of Support, and Biographical Sketches. Carefully proofread all documents and convert them to PDF files.

>> If you encountered any obstacles in obtaining the required documents, devise alternatives to your original plan. You may need to seek out additional vendors for quotations or reduce the scale of your project. Don't hesitate to ask your connections, such as your consultants and collaborators, for help if you run into a last-minute problem.

7.3. Write your Facilities & Other Resources and Equipment sections.

Now that you have fully outlined the scope of your project, it should be straightforward to write your Facilities & Other Resources and Equipment sections. The purpose of these sections is to demonstrate that your company has the physical space and equipment necessary to complete the project. Well-written Facilities & Other Resources and Equipment sections are particularly important for a small company because they validate your ability to accomplish the research outlined in your proposal.

>> Write your Facilities & Other Resources section.

□ Read the instructions for completing the Facilities & Other Resources section, located in the *R&R Other Project Information Form* section of the Application Guide.

□ Provide a detailed description of the space you have available to complete the project. Include your laboratory and office space square footage, special capabilities (such as a laboratory that is specially designed for your project), and other resources that are available, such as shared or fee-for-service facilities. It is also helpful to describe how your location will contribute to the success of your project. If your company is located in an incubator or affiliated with a university or collaborators who can help provide resources, you should state this. If you are in a facility that provides special business, equipment, or library support, make sure to mention this as well. If there are substantial resources required for your project, such as high-powered computing or scientific instrumentation, be very specific about the resources that you will have access to and their capabilities. Ideally, you will portray that your business benefits from the nimbleness of a small entity while also having access to all necessary equipment and expertise to conduct the proposed project.

□ If you do not currently have a laboratory space but plan to move into a space once the grant is awarded, describe the space you will be acquiring. You should have a location lined up where you can do the work, and you should have negotiated the terms of the lease agreement. It can also be beneficial to include a Letter of Support from the location where the work will be performed.

□ If you are working with collaborators, list their facilities in separate section(s) of the document.

□ Refer again to the Scored Review Criteria listed in the "Application Review Information" section of your FOA. Read the questions listed under the "Environment" subheading. Make sure your Facilities & Other Resources section fully addresses all of the points the reviewers will use to evaluate whether the infrastructure you have available will facilitate successful completion of your project.

□ Save and proofread the document, convert it to a PDF file, and then upload it to the Facilities & Other Resources section of the "Other Project Information" tab in ASSIST.

>> Write your Equipment section.

□ Read the instructions for completing the Equipment section, located in the *R&R Other Project Information Form* section of the Application Guide.

□ If you have a laboratory, walk through it and write down all relevant equipment you will use for the project.

□ Write your Equipment section, listing each equipment item on a separate line. If you are planning on purchasing additional equipment prior to the start of the project, list these items as well and write "to be purchased prior to start of project" after each of these items.

□ If you are collaborating with other institutions, list the equipment available at each facility in separate section(s) of the document.

□ Save and proofread the document, convert it to a PDF file, and then upload it to the Equipment section of the "Other Project Information" tab in ASSIST.

7.4. Prepare your Budget.

In Week 2, you prepared a rough budget. You should be able to finalize your budget this week. The Application Guide is particularly helpful in walking you through your budget preparation, and you should follow the instructions in the Application Guide very carefully. Your PO is an excellent resource if you have any questions as you prepare your budget.

The funds you will receive come in three "buckets". First, you will receive funding for direct costs that are directly applied to the research expenses associated with your project. You will also receive funding for indirect costs, which may be used to fund other "allowable" general and administrative company activities, including facility rental and overhead expenses. Finally, you will receive a small amount of funding in the form of a fee, which may be used for any corporate expenses, including patent filing and commercialization expenses.

Your total NIH Phase I award budget will typically be approximately $250,000, unless you have identified a special topic that you are addressing that allows you to exceed the budget cap. It is standard in Phase I to request indirect costs equal to 40% of your direct costs and a fee equal to 7% of your direct + indirect costs. If you plan to apply for a $250,000 award, you may maximize your more flexible funds (i.e., the indirect costs and fee) by requesting exactly $166,889 for direct costs; $66,756 for indirect costs; and $16,355 for a fee. Of course, you may request less than the full $166,889 in direct costs (prior sections of this book have assumed an approximate direct cost request of $150,000), in which case you should modify your indirect costs and fee appropriately. It is unusual to exceed 40% in indirect costs for a Phase I proposal (unless you already have a negotiated indirect rate with the government), and you may not exceed the 7% fee.

A common error is for companies to underestimate the amount of indirect funds and fee that will be required for the company's administrative expenses. Perhaps you have been a virtual company to this point and have a very low overhead. However, once your company receives federal funding through the SBIR/STTR program or other mechanism, you will be subject to a number of administrative, reporting, and financial control requirements. We recommend allocating a minimum of $10,000 - $15,000 to cover the costs associated with your grants management and accounting for a Phase I SBIR/STTR award, and we also strongly recommend engaging a firm with expertise in grant accounting and compliance to ensure these tasks are completed properly. In addition, you will need to set aside funds for attorney costs, office/lab rental, administrative support, travel not related to the project, and many other expenses that cannot be covered with your direct costs.

>> Complete the Research & Related Budget form.

□ Read the entire *R&R Budget Form* section in the Application Guide.

□ Log in to ASSIST and locate the application that you initiated in Week 6. To begin your budget, click the "R&R Budget" tab to navigate to the budget form, and then click "Edit." For an SBIR/STTR Phase I, you typically will need only one project period – Period 1, which is shown automatically.

□ Fill out the Senior/Key Person section of the form, starting with the PI. Click on "Edit" in the table next to the PI's name to enter the necessary information. To add additional Sr/Key individuals, click on "Add Sr/Key Person". Estimate the number of months each senior/key person will dedicate to the project. Be realistic about the amount of time each person will need to devote to the project, as reviewers will check to make sure you justify the time that will be required. We usually recommend that you only include costs associated with salaries; benefits are typically part of small businesses' indirect costs.

☐ Fill out the Other Personnel section of the form, if applicable. For a Phase I proposal, other personnel generally consist of technicians who will help conduct the studies. It is not necessary to include other personnel in Phase I if your senior/key personnel are able to complete all the work.

☐ Fill out the Equipment, Travel, and Participant/Trainee Support Costs in the form. These are often left blank for a Phase I project unless you need to purchase an equipment item or if you need to travel to a collaborator's site.

☐ Fill out the Other Direct Costs section of the form. Make sure you budget plenty of funds for Materials and Supplies, as your project will often require extra materials to work through experimental difficulties. Match up each consultant's budgeted expense with the commitment stated in the consultant's Letter of Support. Enter expenses for studies to be performed by CROs in the blank items in this section (items F8 through F10). In the box for the description, enter the name of the CRO and a brief description of the work to be performed. Then enter the cost in the box next to the description. If you have more than three CRO costs to enter, you can combine the costs into a single item entry. SBIR/STTR proposals usually will not include Publication Costs or Alterations and Renovations.

□ If you have a subaward (required for an STTR grant), enter the total subaward amount in the appropriate box. You will attach the detailed <u>R&R Subaward Budget</u> form, which includes your collaborating research institution's budget and justification, in the "R&R Subaward Budget" tab.

□ If your total budget for direct costs comes out higher or lower than you had expected, you will need to modify your expenses. One of the easiest categories to adjust your budget by a small amount is that for Materials and Supplies. If you need to change your budget by larger dollar amounts, you may consider adjusting the person-month efforts of your personnel.

□ Calculate your indirect costs and fee, and ensure your total budget is less than or equal to the relevant budget cap.

□ Write your Budget Justification. This document is important to justify the NIH's investment in your project. The Budget Justification does not have a page limit, so you may use as much space as you need to convince reviewers that the funds will be well spent. The Budget Justification is usually 2-3 pages in length and should include separate justifications for each line-item expense in your budget. For each of the personnel, state how the individual will contribute to the project and justify the months of effort. You may also reiterate the expertise of each of the personnel in this section, which can help your score on the "Investigator(s)" criterion of the review. Save your Budget Justification as a PDF file, combine it with all the quotations, and attach the combined file to your application. If you are missing any quotations or budget documents from partnering institutions, you should continue to collect these items and add them when they are available.

>> Complete the R&R Subaward Budget form (if applicable).

□ If you have received a R&R Subaward Budget form from a partnering institution, you can select to upload the completed form by selecting "Attach a subaward form". If the partnering institution provided you with budget information in a different format, you will need to select "Add New Subaward" and then transfer the budget information into the application form.

□ Be sure that the partnering research institution's budget justification is included. If the subaward institution provided you with a completed R&R Subaward form to upload, then the budget justification should be located at the end of the year 1 project period. If you are populating the budget for the subaward, then you will upload the institution's budget justification at the bottom of the budget for year 1.

7.5. Complete each of the following sections as-needed for your proposal: Vertebrate Animals, Human Subjects, Authentication of Key Biological and Chemical Resources, Select Agents, Resource Sharing Plan, and Multiple PD/PI Leadership Plan.

Use the following table to determine which of the documents you need for your proposal and then follow the subsequent instructions to complete each required document.

Document	Required when...
Vertebrate Animals	See Week 3.
Human Subjects	See Week 3.
Authentication of Key Biological and Chemical Resources	Your proposed project involves the use of chemical and/or biological resources that can vary over time or between laboratories, are integral to the studies, and/or vary in quality.
Select Agents	Your studies involve the use of select agents or toxins (i.e., biological agents and toxins that have been determined to have the potential to pose a severe threat to public health and safety, to animal and plant health, or to animal or plant products) as defined by the Centers for Disease Control and Prevention (CDC).
Resource Sharing Plan	1) You are requesting $500,000 or more in direct costs, exclusive of the subaward Facilities and Administrative (F&A) costs, in any budget period; 2) You are proposing to develop model organisms; or 3) you are proposing to generate large-scale genomic data.
Multiple PD/PI Leadership Plan	You have more than one PI (or PD – Program Director) for your proposed project.

>> Complete the Vertebrate Animals sections.

□ If vertebrate animals are included in your proposed work, check "yes" for the question "Are Vertebrate Animals Used?" on the Research & Related Other Project Information form in your application. If you are not using vertebrate animals, check "no" for this question.

□ If you are using vertebrate animals, address the questions about Institutional Animal Care and Use Committee (IACUC) review and the Animal Welfare Assurance Number on the

Research & Related Other Project Information form. Instructions for this section are in the *R&R Other Project Information Form* section of the Application Guide. In our experience, the most straightforward way to handle these questions is to indicate that IACUC approval is pending and supply "NONE" for the Animal Welfare Assurance Number. You can then provide this information when requested by the NIH at time of award.

□ If you are using vertebrate animals, write the Vertebrate Animals section to include in the <u>PHS 398 Research Plan</u> form. Follow the guidelines for addressing each of the three criteria listed under the *Vertebrate Animals* subheading in the *PHS 398 Research Plan Form* section of the Application Guide. These descriptions should only include portions of the work that will be conducted on living animals. Procedures for the processing of harvested animal tissues should not be included. Identify the species, strains, ages, sex, and total numbers of animals by species to be used in the proposed work. Be sure to include a power analysis to justify the number of animals you plan to use per group. Additionally, NIH prefers that both male and female animals are used in order to address sex as a biological variable, as long as the disease indication is relevant to both sexes. If dogs or cats are proposed, provide the source of the animals. Second, provide justification that the species are appropriate for the proposed research, and explain why the research goals cannot be accomplished using an alternative model. Third, describe the interventions, including analgesia, anesthesia, sedation, palliative care, and humane endpoints for euthanasia that will be used to minimize discomfort, distress, pain, and injury. If you are uncertain how to address any of these criteria, it is to your advantage to consult with someone who has experience with preparing these documents. The reviewers will evaluate your Vertebrate Animals section, and any serious animal welfare concerns could prevent your proposal from being funded.

☐ Save and proofread the Vertebrate Animals document, convert it to a PDF file, and attach it to your application in ASSIST in the "Vertebrate Animals" section under the "Research Plan" tab.

>> Complete the Human Subjects sections of the application.

☐ Follow the instructions in the *R&R Other Project Information Form* section in the Application Guide for the scenario that applies to your use of human subjects. At a minimum, you will need to answer "yes" or "no" to the first question pertaining to human subjects on the <u>Research & Related Other Project Information</u> form.

☐ If your project involves human specimens and/or data, but does not meet the NIH definition of "Human Subjects Research," you will need to provide a short document titled "Non-Human Subjects" that explains why the application does not involve human subjects. If you are not sure whether your proposed project is human subjects research, the NIH has developed a Decision Tool (Research Involving Private Information of Biological Specimens), available online, that can help you make this determination. For projects using de-identified human specimens or data (e.g., from a biorepository or an existing database), generally a paragraph of explanation is sufficient. Make sure to specify that the samples/data you will receive will be de-identified and include the following information, if applicable to your project: name of the biorepository or database, name of its director/manager, location of the biorepository, any existing IRB approvals covering the biorepository, and any information about the donors of specimens (e.g., age, disease state) that you will receive along with the specimens. It is recommended that you also include a Letter of Support from the director/manager of the biorepository or database as confirmation that the specimens or data will be available for your project.

□ If your project involves the study of specimens and/or data collected from living individuals, either for the purpose of this study or not, you should select "yes" to Human Subjects if the recipient readily ascertains the identities of the individuals to whom the biospecimens/information pertain. The next question asks whether your research is exempt from Federal Regulations regarding Human Subjects research. If you are unsure whether your research is exempt, consult the NIH's Human Subjects Research Infographic for guidance. The Human Subjects Decision Tool may also provide you with information on whether your study is exempt and under which exemption it may fall. If your research is exempt, select yes and indicate the appropriate exemption. If your research is not exempt, select no. For all Human Subjects studies, whether they are exempt, non-exempt, or clinical trials, you should follow the instructions under *PHS Human Subjects and Clinical Trials Information* in the Application Guide. You will then need to respond to several questions regarding the IRB for your study. If your IRB review has not been completed, click yes to indicate that your IRB review is pending, and leave the IRB approval date blank. If you have a Human Subject Federalwide Assurance (FWA) number on file with OHRP, enter the 8-digit number. If you do not have a Human Subject Assurance number, enter "None".

▢ If you selected "yes" to Human Subjects, then you will need to proceed to the "Human Subjects and Clinical Trials" tab. Carefully read the *PHS Human Subjects and Clinical Trials Information* in the Application Guide for detailed instructions. For each separate Human Subjects study or clinical trial, you will need to create a separate "Study Record". Each study record contains five sections:

1. Basic Information
2. Study Population Characteristics
3. Protection and Monitoring Plans
4. Protocol Synopsis
5. Other Clinical Trial-related Attachments

If your project involves human subjects and is not considered a clinical trial, you will need to provide information for Sections 1, 2, and 3. If your proposal is classified as a clinical trial, you will also need to provide information for Section 4. Section 5 is only required when specified in the funding opportunity announcement. Most SBIR/STTR proposals will not require anything for this section. A summary of requirements for each section is provided below:

Section 1 - Basic Information

• <u>Study Title</u>: Select a name for the study. Be sure that it enables reviewers to easily cross-reference the study's location in the Research Plan, especially if you have multiple human subject studies in your proposal.

• <u>Is this Study Exempt from Federal Regulations?</u>: If you are unsure whether your research is exempt, consult the NIH's Human Subjects Research Infographic for guidance.

• Exemption Number: Provide the human subjects research exempt number.

• Clinical Trial Questionnaire: Complete the questionnaire. Note that if you answer "Yes" to all the questions in the Clinical Trial Questionnaire, this study meets the definition of a clinical trial.

Section 2 - Study Population Characteristics

• Conditions or Focus of Study: Briefly describe the purpose of the study.

• Eligibility Criteria: Describe the inclusion and exclusion criteria for the study.

• Minimum and Maximum Ages for Enrollment: Specify the required ages of subjects.

• Inclusion of Individuals Across the Lifespan: Provide scientific justification for the exclusion of any age group and provide a rationale for the minimum and maximum ages selected for the study. Also, discuss the expertise of the team and the appropriateness of the facilities for the specified age.

• Inclusion of Women and Minorities: Provide scientific justification of the inclusion or exclusion of women and minorities.

• Recruitment and Retention Plan: Briefly describe how you intend to recruit subjects for the study and any strategies that will be used to ensure that subjects complete the study.

- <u>Study Timeline</u>: Generate a high-level timeline of the proposed study. This can be in paragraph form or a table/figure.

- <u>Date of Enrollment of First Subject</u>: Select the date that you intend to begin enrollment.

- <u>Inclusion Enrollment Report</u>: Populate the provided table with expected population demographics for study.

<u>Section 3 - Protection and Monitoring Plans</u>

- <u>Protection of Human Subjects</u>: This is a carefully scrutinized document in your Human Subjects section. The document is typically several pages long and consists of Risks to Human Subjects, Adequacy of Protection Against Risks, Potential Benefits of the Proposed Research to Human Subjects and Others, and Importance of the Knowledge to be Gained. Given the high level of detail that you need to include in this section, we strongly recommend that you carefully read the instructions in the *PHS Human Subjects & Clinical Trials* section of the Application Guide, under the subheading *Protection of Human Subjects*, to ensure you include all required details. Also, we recommend asking an individual who is familiar with Human Subjects requirements for NIH projects to review this section of your proposal.

- <u>Single Institutional Review Board (sIRB)</u>: If your study is a multi-site study that will use the same protocol to conduct non-exempt human subjects research at more than one domestic site, you are expected to use a single Institutional Review Board (sIRB) to conduct the ethical review required by HHS regulations for the Protections of Human Subjects Research. You will need to attach a sIRB plan.

• <u>Data and Safety Monitoring Plan</u>: Describe what information will be monitored and the overall framework for safety monitoring, including individuals who will be responsible for monitoring, the frequency of the monitoring and plans for interim analysis, and the process by which adverse events and other issues will be reported.

• <u>Overall Structure of the Study Team</u>: Describe the organizational structure of the team for the clinical trial. This should include any of the following that are relevant to the proposed trial: administrative sites, data coordinating sites, enrollment/participating sites, and laboratory/testing centers.

<u>Section 4 - Protocol Synopsis</u>

• <u>Detailed Description</u>: Describe the study protocol, including assignment of individuals, delivery of interventions, and statistical design and power.

• <u>Intervention</u>: Provide a name and description for each intervention, limited to 1,000 characters.

• <u>Outcome Measures</u>: For each primary and secondary endpoint, provide an endpoint name, the time frame for collection, and a brief description of the metric.

• <u>Statistical Design and Power</u>: State the number of subjects that you anticipate enrolling, the expected effect size, the power, and the statistical methods that will be employed with respect to each outcome measurement that you listed. Justify that your methods for sample size and data analysis are appropriate.

• Participation Duration: Provide the time it will take for an individual participant to complete the study.

>> Prepare the Authentication of Key Biological and/or Chemical Resources section for the PHS 398 Research Plan form.

☐ Read the instructions for the Authentication of Key Biological and/or Chemical Resources in the *PHS 398 Research Plan Form* section of the Application Guide. If your proposed project will use or develop key resources as defined in the instructions or in the table at the beginning of this task, you must describe the methods you will use to ensure the identity and validity of these resources. For example, if your project makes use of a purified protein or nucleic acid that you produce in-house, you may wish to indicate or describe any functional assays that you use to verify the bioactivity of a new batch. Likewise, you might describe the tests specialty reagents (e.g., non-commercial antibodies) must pass before you deploy them in experiments. It is also recommended to broadly indicate which reagents you will purchase commercially and to refer briefly to the QC practices of your vendors. Although the length and details of the Key Resources document may vary considerably between projects, a one-page description of accepted methods for ensuring the quality and identity of research tools is generally acceptable.

☐ If your study does not involve any Key Biological or Chemical Resources that require authentication, you may upload a document to this section that states "not applicable".

>> Prepare the Select Agents section of the <u>PHS 398 Research Plan</u> form.

☐ "Select agents" are certain biological agents and toxins defined by the CDC, and the list of select agents may be accessed through the CDC website by searching for "Select Agents and Toxins List." If you are using a select agent, you must address the three points detailed in the *PHS 398 Research Plan Form* section of the Application Guide, under the subheading *Select Agent Research*. Once you have completed this information, save the document as a PDF file, and upload the attachment to the <u>PHS 398 Research Plan</u> form in ASSIST. If you are not using any select agents, you may leave this section blank.

>> Prepare the Resource Sharing Plan section of the <u>PHS 398 Research Plan</u> form.

☐ For each of the sections in this document that are listed below, you can either provide the information if it applies to your proposal or indicate "not applicable".

☐ The Resource Sharing Plan is divided into three sections, as outlined in the *PHS 398 Research Plan Form* section of the Application Guide, under the subheading *Resource Sharing*:

• <u>Data Sharing Plan</u>: If you are requesting more than $500,000 in a single budget period, you will need to describe how you will facilitate data sharing related to the project. This can involve giving presentations at certain conferences and/or publishing in peer-reviewed journals. The Small Business Act permits SBIR/STTR grantees to withhold data for 4 years after the end of the grant award in order to file patents, which you can state in your plan.

• <u>Sharing Model Organisms</u>: This is required for projects that propose to develop a model organism. You should describe the plans for sharing and distributing the model or state why you cannot share it. You may reference the Small Business Act as a reason for delaying sharing of information.

• <u>Genomic Data Sharing</u>: If you will generate large amounts of genomic data, you should describe your plans for sharing this information.

>> Prepare the Multiple PD/PI Leadership Plan document for the <u>PHS 398 Research Plan</u> form.

□ This document is only required for proposals that have multiple key personnel who are serving in the role of PI as indicated by selecting "PI" as role on the "Sr/Key Personnel" tab in ASSIST. The decision to have a single PI versus multiple PIs is generally based on the experience of the investigators. If your company PI has limited experience managing projects similar in scope to what you are proposing, it may be helpful to include a co-PI with more experience. A Multi-PI arrangement is also common when the expertise of two or more individuals is equally critical to the project. If you are submitting an STTR, the PI for the subaward can either be a co-PI or a co-Investigator. A Multiple PD/PI Plan is needed for a co-PI, but is not needed for a co-Investigator.

□ Title the document "Multiple PD/PI Leadership Plan." The document is usually ½ - 1 page long and should include the following headings and content, as outlined in the *PHS 398 Research Plan Form* section of the Application Guide, under the subheading *Multiple PD/PI Leadership Plan*:

- <u>Rationale for Multiple PD/PI Plan</u>: Describe the expertise of each PI and why a Multi-PI approach is critical to the execution of the project.

- <u>Governance and Structure of the Leadership Team</u>: Describe how often the team will meet to discuss the project and how decisions will be made and agreed upon. Indicate responsibilities for scientific and administrative aspects of the project. Provide procedures for resolving potential conflicts. You may want to indicate that in event of conflict, the company PI will make the final decision, since she/he will have the greatest vested interest in fulfilling the objectives of the SBIR/STTR project, namely commercializing the product.

>> Once you have completed these additional documents as needed, double-check to make sure you have filled out the necessary information in <u>both</u> the <u>Research & Related Other Project Information</u> form and the <u>PHS 398 Research Plan</u> form in ASSIST. It can be confusing that the required inputs for these sections are spread out across both of these forms.

You have spent much of this week wrapping up your budget and additional administrative items while you wait for your reviewers to provide feedback on your Research Plan. Be sure to check in with your reviewers periodically throughout this week to confirm that they are on track to complete their task in a timely fashion so that you are able to produce a final draft of your Research Plan next week.

WEEK 8
Time required: 15 hours

Objectives

This is perhaps the most important week in the proposal preparation process. You will be polishing your Research Plan and writing your Project Summary, which is a document that each member of the SRG will review. You should be very detail oriented this week to ensure your proposal and Project Summary convey the most important points about why your project should be funded. You will also write your Project Narrative and fill out the PHS Assignment Request form, which will complete all of the major documents required for submission.

Tasks

8.1. Make final corrections to your Research Plan.

8.2. Write your Project Summary.

8.3. Write your Project Narrative.

8.4. Fill out the PHS Assignment Request form.

8.1. Make final corrections to your Research Plan.

By now, you should have received feedback from your reviewer(s), preferably both in written format and through a follow-up teleconference or meeting. You may have received feedback from reviewers that you do not agree with, or that you do not wish to implement. It is important to realize that if you feel your reviewer just "didn't understand" sections of your proposal, then it is highly likely that the reviewers in your SRG will have the same impression. Therefore, make every effort to address each point that your reviewers make, even if it involves further clarification of content that you felt was already clear.

>> Address all of your reviewers' comments and create a final draft of your Research Plan.

☐ If your proposal is over the page limit, ensure you are maximizing space by using 0.5-inch margins on all sides and using the smallest possible font size. Your figure legends may have smaller font than your main text, which can save you some space. If you still cannot fit everything into the allotted space, ask your reviewers if they found any areas of redundancy that you could potentially remove.

☐ Carefully and systematically conduct a final review of your proposal. Ensure your figures are sequentially numbered and that the text refers to the correct figure. Make sure you have entered the references in a consistent format. This is a good time to have someone who has not yet looked at your proposal give it a final read, as they may catch additional mistakes with formatting or content.

☐ Once you have completed the final draft of your proposal, save the document as a PDF file. Make sure all figures have saved properly in the file. Then, split the document into three separate PDF files. The first file is your single Specific Aims page. The second file is your six-page Research Strategy. The third file is your Bibliography & References Cited document.

☐ Attach each file in the appropriate section of the application in ASSIST. The Bibliography & References Cited attachment is located on the <u>Research & Related Other Project Information</u> form. The Specific Aims and Research Strategy attachments are located on the <u>PHS 398 Research Plan</u> form.

If you are confused as to why the Research Strategy is attached to a separate form than the Bibliography, you are not alone! However, these sections will be automatically placed next to each other once you submit your application so that the reviewers can easily access your references as they read your Research Strategy.

8.2. Write your Project Summary.

The Project Summary may contain a maximum of thirty lines of text. Other than the three reviewers specifically assigned to carefully review your proposal, most reviewers will not have the time to read every page of your proposal. However, <u>all</u> reviewers on the panel will read your Project Summary. The reviewers will rely on your Project Summary to learn about the Significance and Innovation of your project as well as the Approach you will take to complete your Aims. Therefore, your Project Summary should present a very strong case to reviewers as to why they should recommend your project for funding.

>> A great way to learn how to write a strong Project Summary is to read Project Summaries from currently funded projects, which you can do through the NIH Reporter website. Search the Internet for "NIH Reporter", and you will be directed to a query form where you can search for funded NIH projects by specific parameters. Limit your search results by choosing the SBIR/STTR funding mechanisms, and then further limit the results by entering keywords related to your project. Read through at least five Project Summaries for Phase I projects so that you obtain a sense of how well-constructed Project Summaries are written.

>> Compose your Project Summary. This section is similar to your Specific Aims page, but should be written at a higher level, as it is more likely to be read by reviewers without specific expertise in your field.

☐ Read the instructions for completing the Project Summary in the *R&R Other Project Information Form* section of the Application Guide.

☐ Begin your Project Summary with 2-3 sentences on the unmet need your technology will address as well as the magnitude of the problem.

☐ Introduce your technology early in the Project Summary and emphasize the innovative aspects of your product.

☐ Present the key development milestones that your Phase I project will address.

☐ Explicitly state your Specific Aims and the metrics of success that must be achieved to advance to Phase II.

☐ Your final sentence should restate the innovative nature of your technology and portray the long-term impact that this technology will have on human health.

☐ Have at least one person review your Project Summary. Your reviewer should provide feedback on whether the Project Summary clearly explains the scope and relevance of your project.

☐ Save your final document as a PDF file and ensure that it contains a maximum of 30 lines of text. Attach the file to the <u>Research & Related Other Project Information</u> form of your application in ASSIST.

8.3. Write your Project Narrative.

Your Project Narrative is a very succinct 2-3 sentence section that describes the public health relevance of your project for a lay audience. This section should not take long to write, and you can review examples of Project Narratives from successfully funded projects on the NIH Reporter website.

>> Compose your Project Narrative.

☐ Read the instructions for completing the Project Narrative in the *R&R Other Project Information Form* section of the Application Guide.

☐ Write 2-3 sentences on the unmet need that your project addresses and how your technology will improve public health.

☐ Ask at least one person to review your Project Narrative.

☐ Save your final document as a PDF file. Attach the file to the Research & Related Other Project Information form of your application in ASSIST.

8.4. Fill out the PHS Assignment Request form.

The PHS Assignment Request form is used primarily to assign your project to an appropriate SRG and NIH IC(s). The PHS Assignment Request form is found in the "ADD OPTIONAL FORM" list that can be accessed through the left-hand menu of ASSIST. It is to your advantage to fill out this form to ensure your proposal is assigned to an appropriate SRG. Note that this form will not be read by reviewers, as it is only read by NIH staff at the Center for Scientific Review (CSR).

>> Read the instructions for completing the PHS Assignment Request form in the *PHS Assignment Request Form* section of the Application Guide.

>> Log in to ASSIST and fill out the PHS Assignment Request form to request assignment to the appropriate SRG and IC(s) that you identified in Week 1.

You have now completed all of the heavy-duty work associated with your application! Week 9 will be dedicated to tying up loose ends, and then you will be ready to submit your application in Week 10.

WEEK 9
Time required: 10 hours

Objectives

You will spend this week ensuring you are ready to submit your application by verifying that your required registrations are in place and that your application is complete and polished. It is important to spend some time on these final details so that all of the hard work you have done up to this point will pay off with a professional, competitive application. Since you are now only 2 weeks away from the final submission date, if any of the items due in prior weeks have been delayed (quotations, Biographical Sketches, etc.), you should be very diligent this week in obtaining final versions of these documents. You will also assemble and systematically review your final application to ensure it is complete and error free.

Tasks

9.1. Verify that your required registrations are in place for submission.

9.2. Collect and complete any outstanding items from previous weeks.

9.3. Assemble and systematically review your final application.

9.1. Verify that your required registrations are in place for submission.

In order to submit your application, you will need to use your eRA Commons and Grants.gov accounts that you established in Week 1. Specifically, you will need your SO account for eRA Commons and your AOR account for Grants.gov. This week, you should log in to each of these accounts to verify that you have the proper credentials and that the passwords are correct.

>> Log in to eRA Commons using your SO credentials. To verify that your account does in fact have SO as a role, check in the upper right-hand corner of the page once you are logged in and look under "Roles". You should see "SO" listed. If you do not see "SO" as a role on the account, check to see that you have logged in with the proper account (not the PI account). You may need to contact the eRA Commons Help Desk to assist with creating an SO account.

>> Log in to Grants.gov using the AOR account information. Once you are logged in, you can verify that it is the AOR account by clicking on "My Account" in the upper right corner of the page and then selecting the "Manage Profiles" tab in the center of the page. You will then see a table that summarizes the profile with the role(s) included as a column. Confirm that "Standard AOR" or "Expanded AOR" is listed as a role. If it is not, review the instructions for registrations in Week 1 and/or call the Grants.gov Help Desk to ensure you have AOR status that will be required for submission.

9.2. Collect and complete any outstanding items from previous weeks.

Despite your best effort to collect all materials well in advance of the deadline, you may find that several required documents have been delayed. This week, it is important to be aggressive in tracking down these documents so that you will have everything that you need to submit your application.

>> Ensure you have each document required for your grant application submission, including the following commonly delayed items:

☐ Biographical Sketches for all senior/key personnel, including consultants and subaward/subcontract key personnel

☐ Quotations from CROs

☐ Subaward budget and letter of intent (required for all STTRs and for SBIRs that include a subaward)

☐ Letters of Support

It is very common for collaborators, vendors, and consultants to use the grant submission deadline as their internal deadline for providing you with documents. Make sure you emphasize that the due date for all documents to be in your hands must be well in advance of the official grant submission deadline so that you have sufficient time to assemble and submit your application.

>> Once you have received all of the Letters of Support, you should compile them into a single PDF document and upload the document into your application in ASSIST.

□ Read the instructions for Letters of Support in the *PHS 398 Research Plan Form* section of the Application Guide.

□ As outlined in the instructions, your Letters of Support file should consist of a single PDF file containing all Letters of Support from consultants, stakeholders, customers, etc. Make sure you have included all relevant documents in this file and add the attachment to the <u>PHS 398 Research Plan</u> form in your application.

9.3. Assemble and systematically review your final application.

Now that you have everything in hand to submit your grant application, you should systemically review each section of your application to ensure that all the information is correct and that all relevant files are attached. Be sure to have the list of outstanding items handy that you created as you populated the administrative sections of the application. Mark these items off as you add them in the following steps.

>> For each form in your application, ensure that all of the starred (*) boxes have been filled in with the correct information. It is a common mistake to use an unallowable filename for an attachment, so confirm that each filename complies with NIH specifications, which can be found by clicking the "Format Attachments" link in the *Application Process* section of the Application Guide, under the subheading *Write Application*.

>> For the <u>SF 424 (R&R)</u> form:

□ Confirm that you have the correct Title entered in the "Descriptive Title of Applicant's Project" box. Double-check to make sure your Title is 200 characters or less, including spaces.

□ Now that you know the final amount of funds you will be requesting, fill in the "Estimated Project Funding" box. Make sure you have included your fee as part of the amount of "Total Federal Funds Requested". In the boxes for "Total Non-Federal Funds" and for "Estimated Program Income", you should enter "0". The "Total Federal & Non-Federal Funds" should be equal to the amount in the "Total Federal Funds" box.

□ Ensure you have checked "I agree" in the box to sign and certify the application.

>> For the <u>PHS 398 Cover Page Supplement</u> form, make sure you have filled in all of the required boxes and double-check that you have included the correct email address for the Applicant Organization Contact.

>> For the <u>Research & Related Other Project Information</u> form:

□ Double-check to make sure you have included the necessary information about human subjects and vertebrate animals, including IRB Approval Date, Human Subject Assurance Number, IACUC Approval Date, and Animal Welfare Assurance Number, if applicable.

□ View each attachment for Project Summary/Abstract, Project Narrative, Bibliography & References Cited, Facilities

& Other Resources, and Equipment. Make sure you have attached the correct file in each case and that the text and figures all appear correctly.

>> The Project/Performance Site Location(s) form was initially filled out in Week 6. Be sure that this form is complete for your company and for additional sites.

>> For the Research & Related Senior/Key Person Profile form:

□ Ensure all Biographical Sketches have been attached.

□ Even though the "Position/Title", "Organization Name", and "Degree Type/Year" boxes appear to be optional, you should complete these sections for all personnel to avoid receiving an application error.

□ The "Credential, e.g., agency login" box must be populated with the eRA Commons login ID for the Principal Investigator only. This box is very important, as Grants.gov and eRA Commons use this information to identify and correspond with the PI on the project.

>> For the Research & Related Budget form:

□ Double-check that all of the expenses on the form are consistent with the costs detailed in your Budget Justification. Add up all the numbers from the Budget Justification and then match them up with the total that is calculated on the Research & Related Budget form.

□ Ensure you have filled in the boxes for "Base Salary ($)" and "Cal. Months" for each person listed on the form.

□ Confirm that you have attached the Budget Justification that includes all of the quotes you collected.

>> For the <u>PHS 398 Research Plan</u> form:

□ View the Specific Aims and Research Strategy attachments to make sure all text and figures are clear.

□ If relevant, review the attachments for Vertebrate Animals, Authentication of Key Resources, Select Agent Research, Multiple PD/PI Leadership Plan, and Resource Sharing Plan sections.

□ For STTR proposals, as well as for SBIRs that include a subaward, ensure that the letter you solicited from your partnering research institution in Week 2 has been attached to the "Consortium/Contractual Arrangements". Note that this is a <u>different</u> letter from the Letter of Support you will include from your partnering research institution's PI.

□ Ensure the Letters of Support file includes all of the relevant letters, including consultant letters. It is common to forget to include a letter, so make sure you check over this file carefully.

>> For the <u>SBIR/STTR Information</u> form:

□ Double-check that you have selected the correct Program Type (SBIR or STTR). Note that the program type you select here must match the Funding Opportunity Title on the top of your application. If you decide partway through the application process to change from an SBIR to an STTR or vice versa, it is not sufficient to just change the checkmark on this page. You must initiate a new application with the correct application package.

☐ Ensure that you have checked the correct boxes for each of the other questions on this form.

>> For <u>PHS Human Subjects and Clinical Trials Information</u>:

☐ Double-check that you have populated all required sections and uploaded the appropriate documents.

>> Make sure you have attached the <u>R&R Subaward Budget Attachment(s) Form 5 YR 30 ATT</u> for an STTR proposal or for a subaward/subcontract in an SBIR proposal.

>> For the <u>PHS Assignment Request</u> form, check the Awarding IC and SRG assignment requests to ensure they are correct.

>> Now that you have checked each form individually, you can perform a high-level error check on your entire application to ensure all of the mandatory parts have been completed. Before an application can be submitted using ASSIST, it must pass a series of system and business validations at both the overall application and individual component levels. Keep in mind that additional errors may still be identified through either Grants.gov or eRA Commons once you have submitted your completed application.

☐ Click on the button "VALIDATE APPLICATION", which is located in the left-hand ASSIST menu, to perform an error check. If the validation checks identify any errors or warnings, they will be listed on the Application Errors and Warnings Results page, which opens as a separate window. Errors must be corrected before ASSIST will allow you to submit your application. Warnings do not have to be corrected before submission, but it is to your advantage to read these carefully and to address them at this stage if possible.

>> After you have addressed any errors and warnings, generate a PDF preview of your entire proposal, with all of its forms and attachments, so that you can review it one last time. To do this, click on the "Summary" tab and then select "PREVIEW APPLICATION" on the left-hand ASSIST menu. Once the preview has been generated, which can take a minute or two, download it to your computer and carefully look through it. If you find any errors, address them before continuing.

Congratulations – you have completed your application and are now ready to submit it!

WEEK 10
Time required: 10 hours

Objectives

This week <u>should</u> be simple. You have already assembled your completed application, proofread all documents multiple times, and just need to hit the submit button. Despite this, it is possible that unforeseen circumstances will cause difficulties during your actual submission process. Therefore, <u>it is critical that you submit your application at least 2 business days, and ideally 5 business days, before the NIH deadline, or you risk not having it submitted on time!</u>

Tasks

10.1. Submit your proposal.

10.2. Review your submitted application in eRA Commons.

10.1. Submit your proposal.

Tip: Schedule a complete workday for your submission. Chances are something will go wrong!

Unfortunately, the process of submitting your proposal is non-intuitive. You will submit your application using ASSIST, and it will be forwarded to Grants.gov, which will perform an initial check for major errors. If there are no errors identified by Grants.gov, your application will be forwarded to the NIH and additional errors may be identified and listed in eRA Commons. <u>Your proposal will not be reviewed as long as there are outstanding errors.</u> Fortunately, ASSIST checks for many of the most common errors and *requires* you to correct them before it allows you to submit your application. This feature greatly simplifies the application process. Nevertheless, it is still possible for errors to occur in Grants.gov or eRA Commons, so it is important for you to carefully track your application as it moves through both systems. If errors are found, you will need to correct and submit your proposal again to obtain an error-free submission.

>> Submit your Grant Application. It is best if you can submit your application during working hours so you can call the Grants.gov or the eRA Commons help desks if needed.

□ Log in to ASSIST using your Company's SO login and open your application. Make sure you have selected the left-most "Summary" tab.

□ Before submitting the application, you must first change its status to "Ready for Submission." To do this, click on the "UPDATE SUBMISSION STATUS" button in the left-hand menu. (Note that this button will not appear on the menu unless you have selected the "Summary" tab.) Select the new status: "Ready for Submission," then write a brief comment in the box and click the "add comment button" or select "continue without adding comment". Any comments added here are for your internal tracking and are not seen by reviewers. Now the "Submit Application" button, which is located next to "Status" on the Summary page, should be active. Click it!

□ A Grants.gov dialog box will open and ask for your username and password. Use the AOR username and password that you created when you registered for Grants.gov. Once you have supplied this information, you will need to wait several minutes for your application to be uploaded. Do not close ASSIST. It is best if you do not use your computer during this time for any other purpose so that you don't interfere with the uploading process. Once the application has been submitted to Grants.gov, a confirmation window will open. At this time, you can close your application. If you have trouble with this step, your computer may be blocking the Grants.gov website. Make sure you choose the option to "Allow" your computer to open the Grants.gov window so that you can submit your application.

You can also monitor the submission process of your application by selecting the link for "Check Submission Status" located next to the status category for the application. If you click "Check Submission Status," you will receive updates as the application proceeds through the various steps of the submission process prior to landing in eRA Commons as an official application. Once a proposal is successfully submitted, you will see "Submitted" for the ASSIST status, "Agency Tracking Number Assigned" for the Grants.gov status, and "Processed" for the Agency status in addition to an agency tracking number. You can click on the agency tracking number to access the complete application in eRA Commons.

□ You will receive an email shortly after you submit your application acknowledging submission receipt. Although the email states that validation may take up to 2 business days, you will normally receive a second email within 30 minutes that states whether your application has error(s) or whether it has been validated and prepared for Grantor agency (e.g., NIH) retrieval.

□ Once your application has been validated by Grants.gov, you will receive an email from eRA Commons, generally within about 30 minutes of the validation. This email will state whether any warnings or errors are associated with your application. Read this email closely, as it details the procedure for correcting any errors/warnings. <u>Your application will not be processed if it contains errors.</u> Your application will be processed if it contains only warnings, but you may wish to correct issues identified in the warning(s).

□ Access your eRA Commons account to view any errors and/or warnings. Click on "Status" and then on "Recent/Pending eSubmissions" to access your application. If your application contains errors, log in to ASSIST, open your Application Package, and change the application status from "Submitted" back to "Work in Progress." <u>Navigate to the "R&R Cover" tab, check the "Changed/Corrected Application" box and insert your Grants.gov tracking number into the "Federal Identifier" box.</u> Then, correct each error. You may also choose to address some or all of the warnings. Resubmit your application using ASSIST and follow it through Grants.gov and eRA Commons. Repeat the above process until you have an error-free application.

10.2. Review your submitted application in eRA Commons.

Once your application has been successfully submitted, you can view the application in eRA Commons.

>> View and verify your entire application.

☐ Log in to your eRA Commons account; click on "Status", and then click on "Recent/Pending eSubmissions". Click on the "Search" button to find your application. If more than 2 days have passed since your submission, you may need to click on "List of Applications/Grants" rather than "Recent/Pending eSubmissions" to find your application. Then, click on your Application ID. A new screen will open, under "Other Relevant Documents" you can click on "e-Application" and "eSubmission Cover Letter".

☐ Review your entire proposal. If you are happy with the proposal, then you are done! If you identify any errors and wish to resubmit your proposal, you will first need to have your SO withdraw the current proposal by logging in to her/his eRA Commons account. Once the proposal has been withdrawn, you may resubmit your corrected proposal using the steps described above.

Congratulations! You have now completed the submission process and probably need a good rest!

POST-SUBMISSION

Objectives

After you submit your proposal, you will have a long waiting period before you know whether your project will be funded (see timeline in the Foreword). There are a couple of items that you should keep on top of during that waiting period to ensure the review process is on-track.

Tasks

11.1. Ensure your proposal is assigned to an appropriate SRG and appropriate IC(s).

11.2. Obtain your impact score and Summary Statement.

11.3. Receive your Notice of Award (or work on your resubmission).

11.1. Ensure your proposal is assigned to an appropriate SRG and appropriate IC(s).

Within approximately 2-3 weeks after you submit your proposal, it will be assigned to an SRG and one or more IC(s). You may receive an email notifying you of the assignment, or you may need to determine the assignment yourself by clicking on your proposal in eRA Commons. Check to see if your assigned SRG and IC(s) are the same groups that you requested in your PHS Assignment Request form. If they are not, and you feel that they are not appropriate alternatives, then you should contact the SRO associated with your application. You can find your SRO's contact information by clicking on your proposal in eRA Commons. (Your SRO may be listed as "SRA" in eRA Commons, which is an outdated title for the position.)

Another useful bit of information that will be posted within several weeks after you submit your proposal is the SRG meeting date and roster. Your impact score will generally be posted within 2-3 business days after the SRG meeting date, so you should mark this date on your calendar to note when your score will be available. Although the roster of reviewers in your SRG is publicly available, you may not contact any of the reviewers. However, the roster of reviewers will be useful if you need to resubmit your application, since you will have a better sense of the audience for your proposal once you know the identity and backgrounds of the reviewers.

11.2. Obtain your impact score and Summary Statement.

Your application will receive either an impact score between 10 and 90 or a score of "ND" for "Not Discussed". The impact score is often posted the day after the review panel meets, but occasionally you may need to wait two full business days before your score is available – which is especially stressful if a weekend falls in between the days. More often than not, even after you receive your score, it will still be unclear whether your score is strong enough for your proposal to be funded. There are two extremes, however, that you may encounter. First, instead of a score, you may see the dreaded "Not Discussed". This means that your proposal was in the bottom half of submitted proposals as scored by the three reviewers assigned to your proposal, and so it was not brought up for discussion by the SRG. If you find yourself in this situation, you will likely need to make major revisions, or change the scope of your proposal entirely, prior to resubmitting. On the other extreme, if you receive a score in the 10s or low 20s, you have a very good probability of receiving funding.

Each IC has a slightly different policy for determining which proposals will receive funding. In some cases, ICs will publish a "payline" which is the score a proposal must be at or below in order to be funded. The NIH fiscal year runs from October 1 through September 30, and early in the fiscal year, paylines are published at a conservative number. Later in the fiscal year, paylines may increase until a "final payline" is established, usually in the spring. Some ICs, particularly the smaller ICs, will not publish paylines, and so it is more challenging to predict whether your proposal will be funded. In this case, you should keep in contact with your PO, who can provide insight as to the likelihood of funding.

Within 2-3 weeks after you receive your impact score, you will receive your Summary Statement, which consists of the reviewer critiques. All Summary Statements will contain strengths and weaknesses identified by your assigned reviewers. If your proposal was scored by the SRG, your Summary Statement will also include a summary of the discussion that the panel of reviewers had regarding your application. The Summary

Statement will be posted in the "Other Relevant Documents" section of your proposal's eRA Commons Status Information page. It is important to carefully read the Summary Statement, since it provides the most relevant feedback you will receive about your proposal. It is helpful to have an experienced eye assist you with interpreting the comments you receive on your Summary Statement. Once you review the comments, you should contact your PO, who can help you navigate the comments and discuss how to address the critiques if you need to resubmit your proposal.

11.3. Receive your Notice of Award (or work on your resubmission).

Approximately 2 months after the SRG meeting, the Advisory Council for your IC will meet to discuss which proposals will be funded. If you received a strong or borderline impact score, this is a good time to contact your PO, who should have a better sense for whether your proposal will be funded. You should be prepared for the possibility that it could take several more months before the final decision on your proposal will be made, especially if the NIH has not yet received its fiscal year budget. However, you should keep in mind that the final date that you can receive funding is September 30 of the NIH fiscal year corresponding to your proposal submission. If you do not receive funding by this date, it is time to work on your resubmission.

Resubmissions. If you need to resubmit your proposal, the key to a strong resubmission is to address each one of the concerns listed on the Summary Statement. While it can be frustrating to have to rewrite a proposal, the good news is that it will take substantially less time to complete your resubmission than it did to complete your first submission. Also, you will benefit from the reviewer comments, which can ultimately help you formulate an improved Research Plan that has a better chance of success. You should work with your PO and/or an experienced consultant to ensure you thoroughly understand the reviewer's concerns about your initial submission. It is important to determine which of the 5 review criteria were of the greatest concern to the reviewers, and then to focus on addressing these areas. It is a common mistake to give equal weight to both major and minor reviewer concerns. However, you should focus nearly all of your attention on addressing the major concerns, and make sure you don't get bogged down with minor issues. In general, concerns mentioned in the panel review are more important than those mentioned by only a single reviewer.

In addition to modifying your Research Plan to address reviewer critiques, you will have the opportunity to submit a 1-page response to reviewers. On this page, you should address each critique and any changes you have made to your proposal in response to the critique. It is not necessary to accept every suggestion the reviewers make, but if you choose not to accept a suggestion, you should carefully address why in your response. As with your original proposal, it is important to have an independent SBIR/STTR expert read your resubmission to ensure you have clearly addressed each of the reviewer critiques.

Receiving an award. The first sign that you are being considered for an award is when you receive an email from your Grants Management Specialist (GMS) requesting Just in Time (JIT) information. Once you receive this email, you should provide the requested administrative information as quickly as possible. Your GMS will work with you to make sure you have appropriate financial controls in place and that your company is eligible to receive SBIR/STTR funding. If you don't have an accountant familiar with SBIR/STTR accounting, this is a good time to find one, since it is very important that you properly account for the federal funds you will receive.

After your GMS has approved all of your JIT information, you will receive your Notice of Award (NOA). This is the time to celebrate, as you have officially been awarded your grant! If this is your first award, you will want to read the "Welcome Wagon" letter for new grantees that is available on the NIH website. This letter provides practical information about your requirements and responsibilities for receiving NIH funding. You should also read your NOA very carefully, as there may be restrictions and requirements that are specific to your award.

Financial controls. Although it would be nice to just receive a check for the awarded funds, the NIH has very careful controls in place to ensure their awards are not mismanaged. On your NOA, you will see the phrase, "This award is pursuant to the authority of 42 USC 241 15 USC 638 42 CFR 52 and is subject to the requirements of this statute and regulation and of other referenced, incorporated or attached terms and conditions." The CFR refers to the Code of Federal Regulations, and 42 CFR 52 covers Grants for Research Projects. The details of the code are complex and consist of aspects such as allowable and unallowable costs, reporting requirements, and other grants management protocols.

In order to receive reimbursement for costs incurred, you will first need to set up an account in the Department of Health and Human Services' Payment Management System (PMS). You will need to properly document all costs that are billed to the grant and calculate the appropriate allocation of indirects and fees to draw down from PMS. There are regular reporting requirements throughout the grant period, and you will also need to submit a final close-out report at the end of your project period. Given the complexities of the award terms and conditions, we highly recommend engaging an outside expert in grants management and accounting who can help you to implement a compliant infrastructure and accounting system. An expert in this space should assist you with establishing corporate Policies and Procedures, a timekeeping system, and a Project Class Accounting system, all of which are required for federal awardees.

It is important to keep in mind that if your company spends more than $750,000 in government grants during a fiscal year, you are required to obtain an independent audit. Once you reach this point, you must have a compliant accounting system and controls in place so that the audit proceeds smoothly. Given that the $750,000 threshold can sneak up on you quickly as you secure more grant funding, it is worth the effort to establish a compliant grant accounting system as soon as you receive your first award so that you don't have to backtrack when it comes time for an audit.

Looking ahead. Shortly after you have finished celebrating your award, you will need to get to work again! You now have the opportunity and obligation to complete all of the studies that you proposed in your Phase I application. As you are conducting these studies, keep in mind the metrics of success that you have listed in your Phase I proposal, and focus your experiments on meeting each of these metrics.

Perhaps the most exciting aspect of winning a Phase I award is that it opens the door to applying for a Phase II award for over a million dollars of additional funding. If the Phase I proposal seemed like a lot of work, the Phase II application process will feel even more overwhelming! So, it is a good idea to start planning for your Phase II application early on during your Phase I project period. You should begin by reading the Phase II application instructions so that you are familiar with all of the requirements of the Phase II application. We have also published a book on preparing your Phase II SBIR/STTR proposal, which contains helpful tips about the timelines and requirements for a successful Phase II proposal.

Final thoughts. We hope you have found that the step-by-step approach outlined in this book has provided you with the tools to submit a competitive NIH Phase I SBIR/STTR application, while still leaving you with enough time to conduct your other business activities during the 10-week proposal preparation period. The effort that you put into preparing a strong Phase I proposal will pay off substantially once you receive your NOA. You will find that receiving an SBIR/STTR award will not only provide you with important seed funding for developing your technology, but will also likely generate additional publicity and investor interest, given the prestige of the award and the rigorous review process that your technology will have undergone.

Finally, we wish you the best of luck not only in securing SBIR/STTR funding, but also in developing and commercializing your innovative ideas. No doubt, those of you who are reading this book will contribute substantially to the advancement of cutting-edge technologies in the United States, keeping our nation at the forefront of innovation and dramatically improving human health worldwide.

APPENDIX

RESEARCH STRATEGY CHECKLIST

This checklist is meant to serve as a practical guide to writing your Research Strategy. Use references liberally throughout this document to support all statements of fact.

<u>Significance</u> (1/2 page to 1 page)

☐ State the problem, the size of the problem in numbers of patients affected, and the cost to healthcare system/society.

☐ Describe current approaches to address the problem.

☐ Explain the limitations of current approaches.

☐ Based on the above information, describe what is needed to solve (or help solve) this problem. This is the unmet need. Underline or bold this for emphasis.

☐ Describe your solution to address this unmet need. Be sure to clearly articulate the impact your solution will have on all aspects of the problem (health, economic, and societal) in comparison with current practice.

☐ Include a sub-heading labeled "Rigor of Prior Research". Describe the strengths and weaknesses in the rigor of the prior research (both published and unpublished) that serves as the key support for the proposed project. Describe plans to address weaknesses in the rigor of the prior research.

<u>Innovation</u> (1/2 page to 1 page)

☐ What is your innovation? Clearly describe it in one concise sentence.

☐ Outline what your product is intended to do, who it is intended for (customer), and what it will do for the world (i.e., how it will address the unmet need).

☐ Briefly discuss the current approaches to solving the problem and clearly describe what attribute(s) differentiate your product from these current approaches. Consider including a table or a figure that highlights this information.

☐ Outline your development plan and what is required to get your product to market. You can also include a figure outlining the timeline and major milestones from now to regulatory approval.

☐ Briefly discuss the market and why you are likely to gain market traction.

☐ Discuss your company's history and intellectual property.

Approach (remainder of 6-page limit)

Overview (~ 1 paragraph)

☐ Begin the approach section by outlining the goal of your Phase I project. Briefly describe the Aims. Close by stating where in product development you will be at the end of Phase I.

☐ It is helpful to include a figure outlining the Aims (with milestones) so reviewers can glance at it and get a snapshot of the whole picture before moving into the details of the Specific Aims.

Team (~ 1 paragraph)

☐ Briefly introduce your team (including PI, key personnel, collaborators, and consultants). Highlight each member's experience and what they will be contributing in Phase I. Limit this description to 2-3 sentences.

Preliminary Data (3/4 page)

☐ Describe your preliminary data as you would in a paper. Include headings, rationale, and enough of a description of methods for the reviewers to know how you did it – with special focus on sample sizes, number of repetitions, statistical analysis, and any other details that highlight the rigor of the experiments.

☐ Include a figure summarizing the data. Include error bars and labels, and make sure the figure and labels are large enough for the reviewer to read.

☐ Include a summary sentence for each preliminary study that clearly describes what the data tell you and why this is important.

Bold or underline this statement to ensure reviewers get the take home message.

☐ Close the preliminary data section with a summary of key details and why this positions you to pursue the Aims of your Phase I project.

Experimental Design (2 to 3 pages)

This is where you will describe your experimental methodology for each Aim.

Start a new section for each Aim.

☐ Describe the rationale/purpose of the Aim.

☐ Create a section titled "Experimental Methods". Describe how you are going to conduct the experiments. Provide enough details to make it clear that you will be performing the experiments with rigor, but balance the need for brevity by not including obvious details. For published methods/approaches, you can refer to the relevant paper(s).

Though your "Experimental Methods" section will be brief, be sure to:

  ☐ Describe all of your controls and sample sizes.

  ☐ Provide a power analysis to justify sample sizes.

  ☐ Describe your statistical analysis plan (or other methods for analyzing the data). Make sure to explain exactly how you will be analyzing the data, and what your criteria for pass/fail will be. You can use a subheading called "Data Analysis Plan" or "Statistical Analysis Plan".

☐ Use a figure to summarize your approach if needed for further clarity.

☐ Include a section on your "Expected Results and Alternative Approaches". Discuss what you expect will happen, what could go wrong, and what you will do if things don't go as planned.

☐ Include a final section titled "Milestones" or "Metrics of Success". Describe your success metrics/quantitative milestones. Use a figure or table to summarize them if that is helpful.

☐ Repeat the above format for the rest of your Aims.

Rigor & Reproducibility (~ 1 to 2 paragraphs)

☐ State how you will ensure that your experiments will be rigorous and reproducible (using proper controls, blinding, appropriate statistical methods, etc.). For example: "We will repeat all *in vitro* experiments 3 times on 3 separate days...". Alternatively, you may discuss Rigor & Reproducibility separately in the context of each Aim. Either way, be sure to emphasize how your experimental design will lead to robust and unbiased results.

Timeline and Conclusion (~ 1 paragraph)

☐ End your research strategy by reminding the reviewer of the purpose of Phase I, the output at the end of the project, and the follow-on Phase II studies.

☐ Bring your project home by reminding reviewers of the significance of your project and what successful development of your product will do for patients, health care workers, and society.

☐ Include a Gantt chart outlining the expected timeline for each Aim or Subaim.

GLOSSARY OF ABBREVIATIONS

AOR: Authorized Organization Representative

ASSIST: Application Submission System & Interface for Submission Tracking

CDC: Centers for Disease Control & Prevention

CRO: Contract Research Organization

CSR: Center for Scientific Review

D&B: Dun & Bradstreet

DOD: Department of Defense

DUNS: Data Universal Numbering System

eBiz POC: Electronic Business Point of Contact

eRA (Commons): Electronic Research Administration

F&A: Facilities and Administrative

FOA: Funding Opportunity Announcement

GMS: Grants Management Specialist

IRB: Institutional Review Board

IACUC: Institutional Animal Care and Use Committee

IC: Institutes and Centers

IP: Investigational Product

JIT: Just in Time

NIH: National Institutes of Health

NOA: Notice of Award

PD: Program Director

PDF: Portable Document Format

PHS: Public Health Service

PI: Principal Investigator

PMS: Payment Management System

PO: Program Officer

R&D: Research and Development

R&R: Research and Related

ROI: Return on Investment

SAM: System for Award Management

SBA: Small Business Administration
SBC: Small Business Concern
SBIR: Small Business Innovation Research
SO: Signing Official
SRG: Scientific Review Group
SRO: Scientific Review Officer
STTR: Small Business Technology Transfer
UEI: Unique Entity Identifier

INDEX